Sikhs & Sikhism in Britain

fifty years on

the Bradford perspective

*Dedicated to the celebration of the
Tri-centenary of the birth of Khalsa and
the people of Bradford who have accepted
the Sikh migrants of fifty years ago as an
integral part of their community.*

Sikhs & Sikhism in Britain

fifty years on

the Bradford perspective

by Ramindar Singh

Bradford Libraries

First published 2000 by
Bradford Libraries
Central Library
Prince's Way
Bradford BD1 1NN

ISBN 0 907734 54 5

The views expressed in this book are those of the author and do not necessarily reflect those of the publisher.

Printed in Garamond by Peepal Tree Press, Leeds

ILLUSTRATIONS

CONTENTS

Acknowledgements

The present publication is the result of my continuously observing the gradual rooting of Sikh communities in Britain and my interest in regularly recording the progress of the Sikh community in Bradford. I started my new life, after leaving Punjab in 1965, in Bradford. Since then I have lived in the district, worked in the city and have actively participated in most of the activities of the Sikh community. Thus in one sense I owe a great deal to the whole Sikh community in shaping the experience upon which this book is based. I have benefited from the first hand knowledge of many friends who have held official positions in the local Sikh organisations, in checking the facts and my observations. It is natural that not everybody would agree entirely with my analysis and conclusions. However, they have been extremely supportive of my initiative to document the position of the community in the city at this point in time. I would like to acknowledge the help of Frances Wood, Librarian, the *Telegraph & Argus* in my search for pictures and Perry Austin-Clarke, the editor, for giving permission to use their pictures in the book.

I would like to record my thanks to Philip Lewis and Govinder Singh Dhaliwal for making some critical objective comments on an earlier draft, which helped me enormously to revise it. My thanks go to Kate Mellalieu-Heycock for all the design work, including the cover. Robert Walters and Jane Heap at the Central Library, Bradford were thorough in their editorial advice to improve presentation. Of course, any outstanding weaknesses are mine. I would also like to record my gratitude to the Arts, Museums and Libraries Services for sharing the costs of publication with me.

CHAPTER 1

INTRODUCTION

The last year of the millennium, 1999, is a very special time for Sikhs. It is also the tri-centenary of the creation of Khalsa, a time of celebration for Sikhs all over the world. Sikhs in Britain are a well-rooted community and have been here for almost half a century now, a period long enough to allow the nature and extent of their social, economic and political integration into local mainstream society and its institutions to be assessed.

The present work is being published with the dual objectives of my personal contribution towards the tri-centenary celebrations and an opportunity to update my earlier work on the Bradford Sikh community. I published in 1978 a brief account of the community based on a small-scale survey. This was enlarged and updated in 1980 and again in 1992. The 1992 edition, entitled "Immigrants to Citizens", examined two questions: to what extent the Sikhs in Britain had integrated into mainstream society, and whether their immigrant orientations had changed sufficiently for them to be considered now as full British citizens. It was written at a time when a major debate in Britain had started questioning the Britishness and 'loyalty' of some sections of British Muslims, in the context of the events relating to the 'Salman Rushdie Affair', the 'Gulf War Crisis, and the establishment of a 'Muslim Parliament'.[1]

The loyalty of British Sikhs has never been questioned, so far. However, there have been occasions when the attitude and behaviour of Sikhs in Britain became the subject of media discussion. The most significant issue to raise public concern in the 1960s and 1970s related to the Sikhs' various campaigns to establish the right to wear turbans as a part of their religious identity.[2] They were accused of demanding 'separate' and, more often, 'privileged' treatment under British law. In the 1980s, the activities of some individual Sikhs, the Council of

1

Khalistan and the pro 'Khalistan movement' youth organisations set up in Britain following the events in 1984 became a matter of concern in Britain.[3] Some of the political activities of British Sikhs may still beg questions about their strong 'home orientation'.

In order to update the account of the Sikh community in Bradford, and to examine the nature and magnitude of changes within the community, and the factors that have influenced the processes of adaptation, it was felt necessary to retain a certain amount of significant data from the author's previous works. The present publication not only updates the basic facts about the Sikh community in Bradford it uses the Bradford experience to examine the broad ways in which the Sikhs in Britain have changed since their arrival. To widen the Bradford experience, literature on British Sikhs, the author's personal knowledge of Sikh communities in other British cities and abroad, and the BritishPanjabi press are used as and where appropriate.

Very little qualitative longitudinal research has been carried out to find the ways in which the British Sikh community has changed. As a part of the ethnographical approach, data from a critical study of Punjabi *mehfals* (informal social gatherings) is utilised as and where appropriate. Informal social gatherings of people of similar background and interest, referred to as *mehfals* in Panjabi, are generally a good window on to their inner mind. In *mehfals* people drop their guards and express themselves frankly, freely and, perhaps, more honestly. Here they express their aspirations, boast about their achievements, and share their common disappointments and concerns. Conversations in *mehfals* may sometimes sound petty, casual, purposeless, almost gossip. However, they do offer an insight into the collective soul of a community. They present a mirror image of the inner thoughts of participants. In the absence of hard evidence from formally structured research, a personal reflection on the changes in the topics of discussion in *mehfals* (observed by the author over almost 34 years) offers a valuable account of changes in the collective thinking of Sikh migrants in Britain. Traditionally *mehfals* provided a forum for light entertainment, gossip and, mostly, poetry reading. In the early periods of immigration *mehfals* normally happened at the weekends in pubs or over a drink in the all-male households. These days they assemble more often on social celebrations in family situations or as postscripts to formal meetings or a prelude to political strategic meetings.

It is contended that the Bradford experience is not unique. It has marked similarities in community organisations, internal politics, styles of leadership and the processes of adaptation and change in other communities in the Sikh Diaspora.

As the book is intended for a wide range of readers, a brief description of the Sikh religion, its beliefs and practices, and key moments in Sikh history are included. It provides a general profile of Sikhs in Britain and the Sikh community in Bradford. It examines the position of Sikhs in contempoary Britain and tries to map and evaluate the changes within the Sikh community in Britain and more specifically in Bradford. Currently, many social changes are not positively viewed by most Sikhs and are perceived as a serious loss of traditional lifestyle and values, and therefore, as damaging. Individual Sikhs are changing and most have changed, but at different paces and in different aspects of their lives. However, their attitudes and behaviour have changed within the redefined boundaries of family and community attitudes, values and norms. These social changes are on-going phenomena.

The book presents an account of Sikhs' position in the labour and housing markets and their levels of participation in British mainstream institutions. It highlights their economic and cultural contribution to the local society. The role of gurdwaras as major multi-functional institutions and that of other community organisations, their politics and leadership, are examined. The main changes in Sikh identity and the factors contributing to these changes are discussed in a critical manner. Relations between Sikhs and other communities in Bradford are described and critically evaluated. The concluding chapter contains, fifty years on, a broad general account of the changes in priorities, preoccupations, and concerns. The way they view their 'native home' and the families left behind, sends a clear message - they are 'here to stay' in the adopted home.

CHAPTER 2

SIKHS AND SIKHISM

Development of Sikhism

Sikhism is the youngest of the major world religions, being about 500 years old. Sikhs are one of the smallest religious groups in India (about 2% of the population) but the largest among Indians in the UK, just over 50%.

The founder of Sikhism was Guru Nanak (1469-1539). He was born in the village of Talwandi, now called Nankana Sahib in Pakistan. He was married and had two sons. At the time of Guru Nanak, the Lodhi Muslim dynasty ruled over India. Guru Nanak described the state of affairs as "like a knife; kings are butchers; religion has taken wings and flown; and in the dark night of falsehood I cannot see where the moon of truth is rising".[1] Furthermore he noted that, "modesty and religion have disappeared because falsehood rules supreme; the Muslim *mulla* (priest)

Guru Nanak

and the Hindu *pandit* (priest) have resigned their duties; the devil reads the marriage vows; praises of murder are sung and people smear themselves with blood instead of saffron".[2]

Guru Nanak was a learned man who wrote and composed a large number of hymns now contained in the *Guru Granth Sahib*. He mostly used Panjabi, the language of common people in the Punjab for his Bani (sacred poetry). He travelled all over India and beyond to Sri Lanka, Tibet, Nepal, Mecca and Medina (in Arabia). During his travels Bhai Bala (a Hindu disciple) and Bhai Mardana (a Muslim minstrel) generally accompanied him. He preached to the people against religious fanaticism, intolerance, meaningless rituals, the caste system and the inequality of women. His preachings involved a critical evaluation of Hindu and Muslim religious practices of that time in India. He preached in verses and sang them with music. He was an ardent advocate of married family life and working for one's living. He spent the last years of his life with his family in Kartarpar (Punjab) discharging his family and community duties.

Guru Nanak was succeeded by nine further gurus. Succession to the Guru's gaddi was not governed by any laws of inheritance but was determined by the sole consideration of finding a teacher best suited to safegaurd and develop the spiritual legacy left by the founder. The lineage of Sikh Gurus and their period of guruship is as follows:

Guru Nanak	1469-1539
Guru Angad Dev	1539-1552
Guru Amar Das	1552-1574
Guru Ram Das	1574-1581
Guru Arjan Dev	1581-1606
Guru Har Gobind	1606-1645
Guru Har Rai	1645-1661
Guru Har Krishan	1661-1664
Guru Teg Bahadur	1664-1675
Guru Gobind Singh	1675-1708

The Sikh gurus were all Hindu *khatri* by caste, one step lower than the top priestly class of Brahmins in the vertical hierarchy of the Hindu caste system .The last, Guru Gobind Singh, died in 1708. Over this period of nearly two and a half centuries the size of the Sikh community grew, particularly in the Punjab and its surrounding areas. The growing influence of the teaching of the Sikh gurus was seen as a threat especially to the prevailing imperial religion, Islam. The increasing interest of Sikhs in social and political issues of their time began to worry the Muslim rulers. They made a number of efforts to check this emerging force, including the torturing to death of the fifth Guru Arjan and the sentencing to death of the ninth Guru Tegh Bahadur.

The contributions of the gurus who followed Guru Nanak to the development of Sikh beliefs, religious institutions and practices as well as to the spiritual, moral, social, economic and political value systems of the Sikh society, are briefly described below.

Guru Angad Dev developed the *Gurmukhi* script for writing Panjabi and made elaborate arrangements for teaching ordinary people. He wrote down the hymns of Guru Nanak and organised the Sikhs into 22 *manjis* (religious centres started by Guru Nanak) under lay preachers. Guru Amar Das became Guru at the age of seventy-three. He is best known for the establishment of *langar*, the free and common kitchen in gurdwaras (Sikh temples). It is said that even the Mughal Emperor Akbar when he came to see him was refused his audience until he would sit with ordinary people to eat in pangat. [3] He also instituted new death and marriage ceremonies for the Sikhs. Guru Ram Das became guru at the age of forty and occupied the seat of guruship for 7 years. He founded the city of Amritsar, which is the principal seat of all Sikh activities, and started the work on *Ram Sarover* (the holy pool) at Amritsar.

Guru Arjan Dev, became the fifth Guru at the age of eighteen and remained in position for 25 years. His major contribution was the compilation of The *Adi Granth* (Sikh scriptures) that contains the works of all previous gurus, his own writings and the writings of fifteen other saints (many from low castes and other religions) whose philosophy and thinking were in line with that of the gurus. He also completed the work on the holy pool and erected the *Harimandir*, the temple in the middle of the pool. The Adi Granth was installed in the *Harimandir* in 1604. The Adi Granth remains unaltered except for the addition of the ninth Guru's hymns by the tenth Guru. Guru Arjan was a friend of the Mogul Emperor Akbar, who was known for his religious liberalism. But Jehangir, who became emperor after Akbar's death, turned out to be a religious fanatic. He arrested the Guru and tortured him to death. He was made to sit on a hot iron plate, then boiled in a cauldron and finally hot sand was poured on his body. He gave his life but did not renounce his religion. Thus he became the first Sikh martyr.

Guru Har Gobind became Guru at the age of eleven. He adopted a martial attitude in order to protect the Sikh community. He started organising and training an army. He had 22,000 horsemen with him. He fought four battles against the Emperor's army but did not establish any kingdom of his own. He was imprisoned once but was released later on. He composed no hymns of his own and died a natural death. His principal contribution lies in introducing martial and political dimensions to the existing largely spiritual traditions established by the previous gurus. Guru Har Rai was only seven when he succeeded to the *gaddi* and lived a short life, almost in peace and quiet without much interference from the rulers. He devoted his time and energy to keeping the Sikh community organised. Guru Hari Krishan became Guru at the very young age of only five and died when barely eight years old.

The ninth guru, Guru Teg Bahadur, became Guru at the age of 43 and remained in position for 11 years. He travelled very extensively to spread the Sikh religion. He wrote many verses. His main contribution, not only to the cause of the Sikhs but to the cause of the whole of Hindu society, is that he gave his own life to defend the religion and lives of Hindus in India. During his period of guruship the Mughal rulers were cruel and intolerant towards other religions. They were converting Hindus to Islam by coercion. Minorities in India were denied all rights to hold property, to occupy high positions, and to ride on horses. They were asked to pay an extra religious tax. Some *pandits* (Hindu priests) from Kashmir approached the Guru for help and asked if he would speak to the Emperor Aurangzeb about his cruel and tyrannical policies against Hindus. He agreed to do so and approached the Emperor. The Emperor remained unmoved and instead asked Guru Tegh Bahadur to become a Muslim too. Guru Tegh Bahadur refused to renounce his religion and was beheaded in Delhi.

Guru Gobind Singh became Guru at the age of nine and occupied the position of guruship until his death at the age of 42 years. A Muslim assassinated him. He was a great scholar and studied Persian and Sanskrit. He produced an enormous body of poetic and other writings, all contained in the *Dasam Granth*. On 13th April 1699, the first day of the month *Vaisakh*, at Anandpur Sahib in the Punjab, Guru Gobind Singh transformed the character of the Sikh community from *sants to sant*

Guru Gobind Singh

sepahy, saint-soldiers. He created the *Khalsa*. He baptised five volunteer Sikhs who came from different castes and called them *Punj Piaras* (five beloved ones). The Panj Piaras came from five different castes, *jat* (farmers), *khatri* (business people), *dhobi* (washermen), *jhir* (water carriers), *nai* (barbers). After baptising the five, Gobind Singh received *Amrit* (nectar) himself from them and hailed them with the new greetings: *"Waheguru ji Ka Khalsa, Waheguru ji Ki Fateh"* (the khalsa are the chosen of God - victory be to God). He ordained all baptised Sikhs to bear five Ks:

> *Kes* - uncut hair
> *Kangha* - a comb
> *Kachha* - specially designed shorts
> *Kara* - a steel bracelet
> *Kirpan* - a sword.

Male Sikhs were required to bear turbans and females were asked to wear a *dupata* (scarf) to cover their heads. All baptised Sikhs were to be given the new common names of *Singh* (a lion) to male persons and of *Kaur* (a princess) to female persons. Four broad rules of individual conduct were prescribed:

> Not to consume tobacco;
> Not to commit adultery;
> Not to cut hair; and
> Not to eat *halal* (meat killed by ritual slaughter).

The creation of *Khalsa* by Guru Gobind Singh, a socio-political organisation based on democratic principles, without any distinction between rulers and subjects, the guru and his followers, men and women, was the major turning point in the history of Sikh religion. He favoured and justified the use of power and the sword to achieve his objectives when other approaches failed. He fought against tyranny and the castes and rituals which divided mankind into rich and poor, high and low, rulers and the subjects. During his lifetime he fought many battles against Hindu rajas and Muslim rulers. His four sons were killed in his campaigns against tyranny.

He ended the line of human Sikh gurus and instituted the Guru Granth Sahib to be treated as the living guru in the future. He advocated the belief in a direct link between the Sikh and the Guru, without the need of mediation by any form of priestly class. Gobind Singh completed the religious facet of Sikhism, commanding the Sikhs to be armed crusaders rather than pacifists.

These 200 years witnessed the growth of Sikhism and its transformation into a religious tradition with a military dimension. According to Khushwant Singh (1966) the two hundred years between Guru Nanak's proclamation of faith (AD 1499) and Gobind's founding of the Khalsa Panth (AD 1699) can be neatly divided into two almost equal parts. In the first hundred years the five gurus pronounced the ideal of a new social order for the Punjab. The religion was to be one acceptable to both Muslims and Hindus. It was to be monotheistic, non-idolatrous and free of meaningless forms and ritual. The social order was to embrace all the people, irrespective of their class and caste origins. The doors of Sikh temples were thrown open to everyone and in the guru's langar the Brahmin and the untouchable ate together as members of the same family. In the second hundred years, the period of the sixth Guru through to the death of the tenth Guru, the martial character of Sikh society was fully developed.

Some Key Religious Concepts
Concept of God: In the opening *shabad* of *Mool Mantra* in Japji, recited by the Sikhs every morning, Guru Nanak explains his concept of God as follows: "There is only one God. He is the supreme truth. He is the creator. He is without fear and hate. He, the omnipresent, pervades the universe. He is not born, nor does He die to be born again. By His grace shall you worship Him. Before time itself there was truth. When time began to run its course, He was the truth. Even now He is the truth. And evermore shall truth prevail". Guru Nanak was a strict monotheist. He disagreed with the Bhagats (saints of the Indian Bhagati Movement) who believed in the reincarnation of God and his Avtars (the prophets). Since God was infinite, he could not die to be reincarnated, nor could he assume human form, which was subject to decay and death. He also denounced the worship of idols because people tended to look upon them as God instead of as symbolic representations. He

believed that God was *at* (truth - the ultimate reality) as opposed to *asat* (falsehood) and mithya (illusion). He not only made God a spiritual concept but also based on this concept the principles of social behaviour which he preached.

Concept of Guru:
The Hindu Bhagats and Muslim Sufis had emphasised the necessity of having a spiritual mentor. Guru Nanak went further and made the institution of the Guru the pivot of his religious system. However, he insisted that the Guru be regarded as a guide, a teacher, not as a God.

Ideal of Life:
According to Guru Nanak the ideal of life should be *raj mein jog*, which means living the detached life of a *yogi* (an ascetic) whilst remaining amongst one's fellow beings in order to achieve enlightenment in civic life. He did not approve of ascetic isolation, or torturing of the flesh as a 'step' to enlightenment. His religion was being a *grisathi* (a householder) and he strongly disapproved of monastic living sustained by charity.

Gurdwara:
A gurdwara is open to anyone irrespective of his/her own religious beliefs. The building is used for religious, educational, social and sometimes even political gatherings. Before entering a gurdwara visitors are required to cover their heads and take off their shoes. The holy book, the *Guru Granth Sahib*, is installed on a raised platform. Before sitting down on the floor within the congregation, people vow to the *Guru Grant Sahib* and place their offerings in front of it. No other forms of worship, except the reading and singing of hymns from the book, are permitted.

Priesthood:
In Sikhism there is no institution of priesthood as such. In a gurdwara any Sikh man or woman may conduct a service. There is no single national organisation which co-ordinates, controls and guides the functioning of gurdwaras in Britain or elsewhere. Each gurdwara has an elected committee, which manages the affairs of

the gurdwara and appoints people, e.g. a *Granthi* to conduct religious ceremonies. However, in India most of the historical gurdwaras are controlled and managed by the *Shromani Gurdwara Parbandhik Committee*, elected under legislation.

Main Teachings of Sikhism: a Summary

Belief in one and only one God.

Three key tasks an individual Sikh should perform routinely are: *Naam Japna* - remembering the name of God; *Kirt Karna* - living by honest labour; and *Wand Shakna* - sharing with others.

Individual worship is a simple daily routine: getting up early; having a bath; saying the prescribed prayers in the morning, evening and at bedtime. The prayers can be said when doing routine jobs. Visits to a gurdwara and the company of *sadh sangat* (congregation) are emphasised.

Eating from *guru ka langar*, the common free kitchen to bring about social equality.

Belief in equal status for men and women.

Everything should be done in the name of mankind and God, and self-achievement should be to serve the community.

Denounce *Karam-khand*-rituals, pilgrimages and idol worship. Sikhism opposes idol worship and prohibits any rituals or ceremonies being followed in worship. Pilgrimages, fasts and self-afflictions find no place in the Sikh religious way of life.

Belief in the oneness of the human race.

Vices to control: *kam* (lust), *karodh* (anger), *lobh* (greed), *moh* (worldly love) and *ahankar* (pride).

Virtues to cultivate: self-restraint, toleration, contentment, devotion to duty / dharma, and modesty.

Sewa - service to the community in physical, mental and material forms.

Leading a married and a working life.

Sikhism and Other Religions

"There is no Hindu; there is no Mussalman", preached Guru Nanak. Religious tolerance is one of the central principles of Sikh philosophy. Sikh theology believes that no religion and no prophet can claim finality. However, it accepts the principle of different approaches to the same truth. Sikhs' tolerance and respect for other religious and social sects becomes evident from the following examples. The Guru Granth Sahib contains the contributions of Hindu as well as Muslim saints. A Muslim saint, Mian Mir, laid down the foundation stone of the most sacred gurdwara of the Sikhs, the Golden Temple (Harimandar Sahib) in Amritsar.

Some Economic and Political Ethics

Sikhism advocates hard work and accepts the dignity of labour. It is against exploitation of any kind. It advocates the socialistic principles of sharing with others. It emphasises honest hard labour for living and sharing one's income with the needy because that is the only true path in life. Service to the community is considered an essential religious duty, which may take any form: physical, spiritual, intellectual, in kind, money, goods etc.

The Sikhs have inextricably blended religion and politics. Sikhism is democratic in nature, an assembly of *panj piaras* (five Sikhs) can give a verdict on religious matters, and *Sangat* can take any major decisions regarding the organisation of gurdwaras.

The use of a sword is accepted in order to protect dharma, the right path for human beings. To fight for justice and against cruelty to mankind is one's prime duty. A Sikh is necessarily a saint-soldier.

Sikhism is against discrimination of any kind based on race, gender, disability, class, caste and so on.

Caste and Social Division

Gurus were ardent advocates of a socialist society, an egalitarian casteless society. They worked to establish a social order where everyone would be equal without any distinctions of caste and creed. *Sabhe Sanji War Sadyan, Koi na dise bahra jeeo,* all should belong to one community without any exclusion, was the central principle behind their preaching. Guru Nanak proclaimed that individual salvation does not depend on one's caste but on one's individual actions. Caste gives pride, one of the vices. Privileges and status based on caste are wrong.

Sikh gurus reject the vertical hierarchy of the Hindu caste system. They advocate the equality of man irrespective of social status by birth or achieved socio-economic status. To reach this objective in social life they introduced a number of religious practices. For example, a gurdwara is expected to have four doors, symbolising its openness to all. *Guru ka langar*, a free communal meal, is eaten together in a gurdwara. In a gurdwara everybody is expected to sit at the same level (on the floor). *Karah Parsad*, the blessed sweet food is distributed to everyone at the end of worship. Such practices were introduced to destroy the concept of purity and caste differentials. The *Guru Granth Sahib* contains contributions of saints from different castes. Guru Nanak, himself a non-Brahmin, became a preacher. However, contrary to these beliefs and practices, caste considerations have survived among Sikhs, particularly in social relationships such as marriages.

Status of Women

In the time of Guru Nanak equality for women was denied in practice. Polygamy and child marriages were common. *Sati*, the burning of a woman on the funeral pyre of her husband, was prevalent. Re-marriage of widows was not allowed. A woman was considered temptation incarnate. Sikh gurus spoke against these customs loudly and clearly. They advocated social, religious and political equality for women with men. The concept of women being basically evil: unclean and seducers was denounced. *Sati* was denounced. Female infanticide and charging of bride price were strongly condemned. A woman was considered as a strength for a man in character building and in the attainment of spiritual heights. Sikhism is against polygamy. One man and one woman is the golden rule. *Pardah* is condemned. Child-marriage is prohibited. Sikh society accepted divorces and the re-marriage of widows long before the Hindu Marriage Law in India was enacted.

Family

Social conventions rather than religion determine the norms in a family. The extended family or joint family is still a common feature of Sikh life. Male and female roles within the family remain traditionally defined. Individuals are respected within the family according to their ordinal position. But the precise nature of these roles is difficult to describe as they are, to some extent, dynamic and continuously being modified.

Marriage

Marriage is seen as the bringing together of two families. It is based on equality in partnership. Only those are truly wedded who have but one spirit in their two bodies. Marriages generally take place in gurdwaras in Britain. They are customarily arranged between the parents. The practice of arranged marriages is traditional rather than religious and has undergone significant changes. The marriage ceremony is called *Anand Karaj* (Hindu Marriage Act 1955).

Births

The birth of a child is hailed joyfully, especially the birth of a boy; the family distributes sweets. There is no specific ceremony connected with birth. When the mother is well enough, the family takes the baby to a gurdwara. The *Guru Granth Sahib* is opened at random and a hymn is read out. The parents are asked to choose any name beginning with the first letter of the first word of the hymn.

Deaths

Sikhs cremate their dead. The ashes and remains are normally immersed in running water. Many ceremonies at the burial are traditional and social, rather than religious.

An Overview of Sikh History

The sixth Guru was the first to appeal to the Sikhs to keep arms; the tenth Guru Gobind Singh put a Sikh army on a regular footing. The intolerance shown by some of the Mughal emperors, especially after Akbar the Great, was mainly responsible for this change. Jehangir, who had grown suspicious of the spreading influence of Sikhism, put Guru Arjan to death in 1606. His son Guru Har Gobind had to undergo 12 years imprisonment in Gwalior. He fought four battles against the Mughal troops and defeated an imperial army of Shah Jehan near Amritsar in 1628. He ultimately retired to Kiratpur at the foot of the Shiwalik Hills. Aurangzeb put Guru Teg Bahadur, who succeeded Guru Har Kishan, to death. His martyrdom infused a new spirit in the Sikhs, and they organised themselves into a full-fledged military force under the leadership of Guru Gobind Singh, the son of the assassinated Guru. Guru Gobind Singh's entire life is a record of glorious heroism and supreme sacrifices. His career as a military leader is significant as the first serious attempt to overthrow the Mughal Empire in the north of India.

On his death he left behind him a trusted lieutenant, Madho Das, who was renamed Banda Singh Bahadur. This valiant soldier wreaked a terrible vengeance on the oppressors of the Sikhs. His boldness and fierceness made Emperor Bahadur Shah outlaw the Sikh community. Banda Singh continued to face the wrath of the Mughal rulers until in December 1715 he was besieged by the Mughal forces and starved into surrender. Some 780 Sikhs were executed at Delhi in March 1761, while Banda Singh was tortured to death. With the rapid deterioration of the Mughal Government at Delhi, the Sikhs began to reorganise their ranks, and a number of powerful chieftains soon appeared. In 1758 the Sikhs occupied Lahore for a brief period, but withdrew with the advance of the Durrani invader. They conquered Sirhind in 1764 and finally occupied Lahore in 1765. In the meantime they had organised themselves into 12 powerful Sikh *misls* or confederacies. In one of these misls, the Sukerchakias, was born Ranjit Singh, who built the kingdom of the Punjab.

Ranjit Singh was a great warrior and a great administrator. Before he died in June 1839, he had succeeded in establishing a kingdom that was large in size and rich in fame. His greatest achievement was in effecting the transformation of the warring Sikh states into a compact national monarchy supported by a modern army.

After Ranjit Singh's death his kingdom began to crumble rapidly. The final collapse came about as a result of the two Anglo-Sikh Wars, which followed each other in rapid succession, when Lord Dalhousie annexed the Punjab to the British dominions in India in March 1849. Maharajah Duleep Singh, who was only 13 years old, was separated from his mother. He was taken to Britain in 1854 where his mother eventually joined him.[4]

For almost one hundred years after the annexation of the Punjab, Sikh politics was largely concerned with establishing Sikhism and a distinct Sikh identity, separate from the Hindus and with the liberation of Sikh gurdwaras from the traditional control of *mehants* (occupiers of gurdwara properties and incomes). The development of the *Singh Sabha Movement*, the establishment of the *Khalsa Diwan*, the *Sharomini Gurdwara Parbandhik Committee* and the *Akali Dal* were integral parts of the same struggle. The Sikhs also remained leading players in nationalistic movements, e.g. *Kuka Movement, Ghadar Party Movement, Jallianwala Bagh Episode, Babbar Akali Movement* and *the Indian Revolutionary Movement* under Bhagat Singh, fighting for the independence of India from British rule.

Since India's independence in 1947, two major issues have been central to Sikh politics: the position of the Panjabi language in the Punjab and the establishment of an independent Sikh state within India. The Punjabi Suba Movement in its different forms in the 1950s and early 1960s brought the Sikhs in direct confrontations with the Punjab state governments and Indian central governments until the reorganisation of Punjab on linguistic bases into two separate states of Punjab and Haryana. The Sikh's struggle for an independent state or a state with Sikh dominance, Khalistan under various names and concepts, is a continuing political issue in India. The impact of this movement within the Sikh Diaspora in the 1980s is discussed in later sections.

CHAPTER 3

GENERAL PROFILE OF SIKHS IN BRITAIN AND BRADFORD

In the absence of a question on religion in any of the census surveys to date in Britain, estimates of the religious composition of people of South Asian origin can only be derived from a variety of alternative sources. Some of these sources are fairly comprehensive and provide reliable figures for general use. However, all available estimates must be treated with the usual caution. The most recent estimate suggests that people of Indian ethnic origin constitute the biggest minority group, 850,000 in Britain.[1] Fifty per cent of Indians and 19 per cent of African Asians are Sikhs.[2] Using these figures, the Sikh population in Britain works out very close to half a million. According to an earlier estimate, nearly three quarters of the Sikhs in England and Wales were settled in the South East and the West Midlands and only about 10 per cent in Yorkshire and Humberside.[3]

A count from the electoral register of the city of Bradford for the year 1977 gave an estimate of about 700 Sikh households, containing about 5,000 people. Another survey indicated that Sikhs constitute 47 per cent of the Bradford Indian population, slightly lower than their representation in the national estimates.[4] From the estimated population of 13,556 people of Indian origin in Bradford in 1996, there would be about 6,400 Sikhs in the city. This is much lower than the popular figure of eight thousand, usually mentioned.

Bradford's Sikh population is virtually stable. All the indications are that it is not likely to increase significantly for four main reasons:

1.   Most of the Sikh girls seem to marry outside Bradford and move out to live in the city of their in-laws.
2.   A majority of the young Sikh boys, particularly those with professional qualifications follow the job opportunities and tend to settle at places of employment away from Bradford.

3.   Most young Sikhs, male and female, are becoming increasingly career minded. This is resulting in marrying late, delaying the start of a family with increasing aspirations for their offspring and also tending to limit the number of children per family.

4.   The family size among Sikhs has decreased and the birth rate is very close to that of the local white population. With a possible increase in the death rate as the Sikh population gradually ages, net addition to it is unlikely.

The average size of Sikh households in Britain decreased from 5.70 to 4.8 during the period 1974-84.[5] The average size of a Sikh household in Bradford in 1977 was 5.4, lower than the national average for the Sikhs. Even though no recent comparable figures are available for Bradford, the situation is unlikely to be different from the national trend.

Like other post-war immigrants into Britain, Sikhs came to this country looking for work. Most of the Sikh immigrants in Britain have their origin in the two districts of Punjab, Jalandhar and Hoshiarpur. It is sometimes argued that emigration from these two districts to other parts of India and overseas had been a tradition and an economic necessity.[6] The 1977 survey established that 85 per cent of all Sikhs in Bradford came from the Punjab direct and others came from the East African countries of Kenya, Uganda and Tanzania. More than two thirds of the heads of Sikh households, mostly men, had arrived in the city by 1967.

The economy of the Punjab is predominantly agricultural and village-based. In these two districts land is scarce, the population dense, and industrial employment limited. Despite the Punjab being one of the most prosperous states in India, life in these districts was hard in the 1950-60s, and economic opportunities were limited for those who aspired to a decent lifestyle. I have argued elsewhere in detail (Singh and Ram, 1986) that the migration of Sikhs from the Punjab does not fit the usual economic scenario of high local unemployment (including disguised unemployment), grinding poverty or persecution in the sending economies. Neither did the partition of the Punjab in 1947, which created Pakistan and a mass movement of populations between India and Pakistan, have as significant an effect on emigration as is commonly argued in the literature on South Asian immigration.

Map of Punjab - Districts

Emigration from the Punjab had been basically the result of three factors: a previous strong tradition of emigration from the area, the presence of profound internal competition among Punjabis for self-advancement coupled with enhancement of their families' social position in the local community, and the process of "chain migration". Together these resulted in large-scale emigration from the middle of 1950s to mid 1960s to Britain. The emigration process developed a dynamic of its own, a kind of chain, linking people from the same family, village or community. In this process the costs of emigration and feelings of insecurity about the destination become less important, social pressures to migrate increase and individual motivations become secondary. More recently, leaving home for other reasons, such as obtaining higher social status within the village community, has become increasingly important. Emigration from the Punjab to Middle-eastern countries in the 1970s and to Canada in the 1980s and the 1990s is a part of the same process.

Initially, a significant majority of the Sikhs who migrated to Britain came from rural areas with backgrounds in agricultural work. It was mainly after the Immigration Act (1962) that professionally qualified teachers and other educated people employed in low to middle range administrative jobs were attracted to Britain. There was also a good number with skills like carpentry, plumbing, and masonry relevant to industrial work in Britain. Those who came from East African countries particularly fell into this category. Again a very small number, largely from small towns, had experience of running small businesses mainly as self-employed artisans or owners of repair shops or retail stores.

During the peak period of Sikh migration to Britain (1955-70) the general level of literacy in the Punjab was low. According to the 1971 Indian Census only 40.4 per cent of the total male population was literate. The author's survey of Bradford Sikhs in 1977 indicated that almost a third of heads of Sikh households had no formal education, only one in five had attended secondary schools, and another third had passed the Matriculation Examination (GCSE Level). The remaining 17 per cent possessed a mixture of post-school academic, professional or technical certificates. It was interesting to note that whilst one in four could not read and write Punjabi, their mother tongue, almost two thirds of the men interviewed could speak simple English.

Bradford did not attract a large number of degree holders and trained teachers from the Punjab, as did places like London, Southall and Birmingham. In 1965 (the year of author's arrival in Bradford) no more than a score of Sikhs with such qualifications could be counted in the city. There were only two Sikh teachers, Gurnam Singh Sanghera and his wife Harminder Kaur Sanghera, working in local schools. Two more, Sadhu Singh Dhesi and Joginder Singh Sahota, started teaching a year later. They were all employed to teach newly arrived Asian children in the Immigrant Education Centres of the Local Education Authority.

Settlement Pattern

In almost every city in Britain Sikh migrants initially settled in the inner city areas where housing accommodation was generally cheap; where access to work was easy and discrimination in the housing market was relatively less evident; and where shopping and other facilities were handy. An immediate consequence of these considerations, however, produced pockets of Sikh concentration within local white communities. For example, in 1977-78, almost three-quarters of the Sikh voters were concentrated in the Bradford North Parliamentary Constituency and the remaining quarter in Bradford West. Within the Bradford North Constituency, Bradford Moor ward contained 42 per cent of the total Sikh voters in the city and the remaining Sikh voters were spread in the four wards of Laisterdyke, Bowling, Undercliffe and Bolton. (Singh, 1978) Another survey carried out three years later (Ram, 1984, Table 13, p. 66) confirmed a similar pattern of distribution of Sikh voters. Sixty two per cent of all Sikh voters (2,855) were concentrated in the northern part of the city in Bradford Moor (1,003), Bowling (362), Undercliffe (193) and Bolton (209). In the West, University (205), Little Horton (290), and Great Horton (132) wards contained 22 per cent of the remaining Sikh voters.

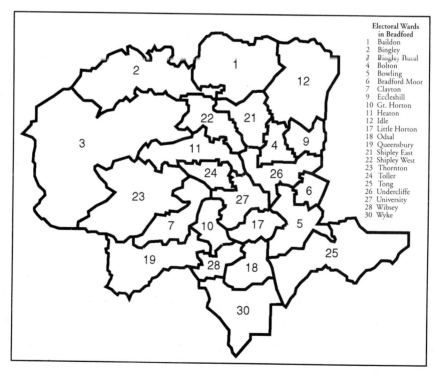

The type of residential accommodation occupied by Sikh immigrants was significantly determined by the availability of a large stock of back to back and terraced houses in the inner city areas.[7] Some of the terraced houses were sound and spacious. Many of these houses were renovated through generous improvement grants. In 1977, nearly two-thirds of the Sikh households lived in terraced houses and only five per cent in back to back houses. Only 30 per cent lived in semi-detached houses away from city centre districts. In general terms the Sikhs were not in a widely different, or worse, housing situation than the general population. Considering the quality along with the housing tenure and the type of housing, the Sikhs were very well placed compared with other sections of the local population. Thirty eight per cent of the Sikh households had central heating and 73 per cent had carpets in all the rooms in the house. Most of them had hot water supply, bathing facilities and an inside lavatory.

With the reunion of Sikh families, considerations in the choice of residence became different. The size and type of house, social status of the district, nearness to schools, and the general environment of the area became the prime factors in house buying decisions. Sikhs in Bradford have gradually moved out of the inner city areas of their initial settlement into residentially more desirable areas. A number of factors has contributed towards this development. They have a clear intention to stay permanently in Britain. The majority of them have a reasonable fluency in spoken English making it easier to live outside the concentration of their own communities. Unlike some Muslim women, Sikh women have a freedom to shop and move about independently which makes it less essential for them to live in the nucleus of South Asian communities, close to ethnic shops. Sikh families are relatively more affluent than, for instance, Pakistani and Bangladeshi families in Britain, as in most families both husband and wife work. Sikh families also have a high level of car ownership which reduces the necessity of remaining close to the place of work.

Ram's research concluded that over the period 1971-80, Sikhs in Bradford migrated out from the inner wards to the urban outer wards of the city. He further concluded that the majority of non-movers in inner wards were also living in good, newer and spacious semi-detached or detached houses. (Ram, 1984, p. 64). For example, they have moved from the triangular area between Otley Road, Leeds Road and Killinghall

Road to Thornbury and further towards Leeds. A significant number of Sikh families have moved into semi-detached houses in Pudsey and into newly built houses off Kings Road and Bolton Road. The movement of Sikh families into better quality accommodation in Bradford fits in with similar observations made in other cities.

The Sikhs seem to have followed the classic path for other successful immigrant groups in Britain, such as Jews, to look for better living accommodation away from city centres. It is interesting to note that even in the case of this outward movement to new areas, Sikhs have tended to move in 'a group of families', indicating that feelings of security and nearness to friends and relatives are still extremely important factors in the choice of residence.

House Ownership

It is generally acknowledged (Smith, 1976; Brown, 1984) that South Asians have a strong preference for buying houses rather than renting them. They believe owning a house is a profitable investment and a status symbol. Owner occupancy among Sikhs in Britain is almost 100 per cent. The quest for outright ownership of sound residential property can be easily explained.

- Living in rented property or council accommodation is perceived as a failure within their immediate social network and therefore, carries a social stigma.
- Owning a house is a good substitute for their customary instinct for land ownership. They do not perceive investment in land in industrial Britain as an income generating source or a status symbol.
- With the gradual realisation of the permanency of their stay in Britain, buying bigger and better houses has become an attractive alternative investment to buying land in the Punjab or building a *kothi* (a big modern brick-built house) in their native villages.[8]
- A very high proportion of Sikh women work for wages. Generally, most men have been in steady employment in the labour market, thus making good quality housing affordable.
- The internal culture of the Sikh community in Britain is so competitive that even those families who lack the financial ability to afford an expensive property tend to furnish their houses with luxuries and keep them in good condition.

· In many families children have achieved a standard of good education and decent professional jobs. For them, having a quality house in a good residential area is a status symbol and a sign of affluence.

The achievement of almost one hundred per cent owner occupancy among Sikhs in Bradford as early as 1977 become possible through the availability of cheap houses, the speedy reunion of families and the large majority's desire to extend their stay in Britain beyond what had initially been intended.

It has also been observed that, more recently, a small number of older Sikh couples have started moving into local council housing accommodation. This is an indication of the changing attitudes of the younger generation towards the joint family system and a recognition, on the part of older people, that they cannot and, perhaps, should not entirely depend on their children in the later years of their lives.

Family Structure and Social Networks
For the Sikhs in Bradford, the all male-households of the 1950s and 60s turned into family units by the mid 1970s. Almost one in three families joined the head of the household in Bradford within a year of his arrival. Others joined within the first five years of the main breadwinner's arrival. In contrast to the case of Pakistanis in Bradford where a five to seven year gap between the arrival of the head of the family and the wife and children was identified as a norm.[9] It can be argued that the rapid reunion of Sikh families in Bradford may be one of the important explanations for their better position in the labour and housing markets. It may also be a key factor in the higher levels of educational achievements of Sikh children compared with children of people of Pakistani and Bangladeshi origin.

The South Asian family structure in Britain is commonly believed to be of a joint nature. In a physical sense a joint family implies the living together of married siblings, or two or more generations living together, or any combination of the two. Even if a South Asian family is nuclear by western standards, that is, husband, wife and children living together, it virtually remains joint in terms of discharging social obligations. This implies sharing the responsibility towards aged parents and grand parents, married sisters and their children, and the wider social group called *'biradari'* or *'bhaichara'* (group of people of the same caste in a village who exchange gifts at social functions).

In the 1977 survey, more than two-thirds of Sikh households in Bradford were nuclear families. At this early stage of settlement such a high proportion of nuclear households among Sikhs came about largely due to the availability of small and cheap houses which encouraged even young married couples to establish their own independent homes. The process was further facilitated by the generous financial assistance normally available to them from parents on both sides. However, these families continued to operate like joint families in fulfilling their social obligations and in maintaining strong mutual relationships. Thus, the functioning of an individual family and its position in relation to the network of social contacts were basically determined by the traditional pattern. To a large extent this situation remains unchanged.

Even after half a century, Sikhs in Bradford are like a village community, close-knit with almost everybody knowing everybody else. Various factors contribute towards the preservation of this strong internal coherence. Despite some spatial dispersal the majority are still settled in small compact areas of the city. On their movement out of the initial area of concentration around Leeds Road, they settled in large groups in the Bradford Moor area in the 1970s, in the Kings Park housing development and in Pudsey in the 1980s and more recently in the new housing estate off Rooley Lane. Most Sikh families have some close relatives or someone from the same village in the Punjab living in the city. Ample opportunities exist for most of them to meet in local gurdwaras at weekends, the focal points for religious, social and other community activities. With a serious decline in the earlier pattern of male socialisation in pubs, the frequent visiting of family and friends has become a favoured activity among Sikhs.

The nature and structure of close-knit village communities has altered as a consequence of migration. Even though from the outside the local Sikh communities look close-knit, the caste, *biradari* or extended network of relatives no longer provides the same cohesiveness within the community boundaries. In this changed structure, the position of elders in Sikh families or even in the wider Sikh community has fundamentally changed: they no longer have a legitimate authority to apply any sanctions to control or punish deviancy. Whereas in the past these elders were the agents of the cooling-down processes when family situations became fraught and boiled over, the young no longer respect their age alone as sufficient reason to heed their arbitration.

The bases for social interaction and relationships within the community have changed too. The significance and strength of relations based on family and 'marriage links' are gradually weakening. New relationships based on personal mutual friendships, without any blood-ties, have given birth to a new kind of *biradari* which operates on the same level as the traditional net-work of relationships. The old style of social politics, concerned with reciprocity of dealings between families and relatives, is replaced by a new kind of social politics between friends.

Social Divisions

The divisions and conflicts within the Sikh community in Britain (or elsewhere) arise from a variety of sources: inter-personal rivalries, caste groupings, class position, membership of a particular sect or the following of a particular *Sant* (saint).

Caste

The presence of caste and class divisions is often described as individual or collective weaknesses. They are perceived as the lingering effects of Hinduism and undesirable facets of social reality, created and maintained by economic and political structures. Despite Sikhism's absolute condemnation of the birth-related hierarchical Hindu caste system, with notions of the social superiority and religious purity of higher castes, caste divisions and caste consciousness among British Sikhs are still intact.[10] On the caste basis, Sikhs in Britain are divided into four main groups.

(a) *Jat*-Sikhs, members of the rural peasantry and the farming community from the Punjab who perceive themselves as of higher social status.

(b) *Ramgarhia*-Sikhs, the village artisans, carpenters blacksmiths, masons, bricklayers, plumbers, tailors etc.

(c) *Ad-dharmi*-Sikhs (Ravidasias), mainly those who were landless agricultural labourers, leather workers or small wage earners in the Punjab.

(d) Urban-based caste groups, largely from business backgrounds.

In the early years of immigration, when the community was mainly male and small in size, caste distinctions mattered little. However, as the families joined and the size of the community enlarged, caste became important simply because the most intimate social interaction, particularly marriages, traditionally take place between the members of the same caste. Caste has also played a significant part in the formation and leadership of community organisations. However, it is encouraging to note that caste does not inhibit free and frequent social mixing between members of separate groups. Although caste consciousness amongst the younger generation is in gradual decline, inter-caste marriages (a social indicator of the changing significance of caste) are still uncommon.

Class

Since their immigration to Britain, members of all caste groups have vastly improved their economic and occupational status but 'class' as a measure of social status within the Sikh community itself has not replaced 'caste' as yet. For example, in Bradford one of the major reasons why *Ramgarhias* and *Ravidasias* split away to establish their own separate gurdwaras was the attempts by *Jat*-Sikhs to exert their traditional dominant position in the management of gurdwaras.

Changes in the social class structure of Sikh migrants to Britain are becoming evident and sharper with their changed occupational positions in the labour market. For example, most *Ramgarhias* have firmly established themselves in the higher levels of occupations, but closely related to their traditional caste occupations.

A significant proportion of *Jat*-Sikhs and *Ravidasias*, particularly, those with a reasonable education, have gone into small retail grocery and off-licence businesses or have bought newspaper shops or post-offices or else have gone into higher status professions. For most of the *Jat*-Sikhs running a business is a complete departure from their traditional caste occupation of farming. Again, for *Ravidasias,* traditionally earning their living through wage labour, running small businesses is a tremendous change in social status. Most Sikh women, irrespective of their caste, have similar job patterns and enjoy an enhanced economic and social status inside and outside the family.

Religious Sects

The cohesiveness of the Sikh community is also affected by the presence of small religious sects. These sects exist on the basis of their differing interpretations of the teachings of the Ten Sikh Gurus and the way they observe religious practices and perform social ceremonies.

The most controversial sect is that of the *Nirankaris*. They have both Hindu and Sikh followers. Initially, the Sikhs considered the movement as a helpful step towards the restoration of the purity of Sikh thought away from the denigration of Hindu ceremonies and idol worship. But the lax attitudes on meat eating, drinking and sexual matters particularly adopted by Nirankari leaders in their own life style have been condemned by orthodox Sikhs. Most of Sikhs now see the whole movement as a part of the 'Hindu conspiracy' backed by the Indian Government to destroy the separate *Khalsa* identity of Sikhs.[11] The movement has its followers in Britain but the scale of its national membership is not known. In Bradford, there are about one hundred active members, both from Hindu and Sikh families. They have established the Nirankari Bhavan in Napier Street, off Leeds Road, where they meet regularly. They keep a very low profile within the community but came temporarily into the lime light when their late chief, Baba Gurbachan Singh, visited Bradford in 1978.

Another Sikh sect, Namdharis (also called *Kukas* or *Kookas*), founded by a member of the *Ramgarhia* caste, Baba Ram Singh (1816-1885) exists in Britain. They fundamentally differ from the Sikhs in having a living guru. The *Akal Takhat,* one of the five seats of Sikh religious authority, also declared them as non-Sikhs. Despite this edict *Namdharis* have remained within the Sikh social community and their membership is largely drawn from the *Ramgarhia* caste. In Bradford there are no *Namdhari* families; however, in Leeds there is a group of families belonging to this sect.

Radhaswamis are another sect within the Sikhs. Unlike mainstream Sikhs, *Radhaswamis* believe in a living guru. They do not stress the *khalsa* traditions and attach more significance to 'Nam-Simran' (recitation of God's Name). Their congregational practices differ in some significant respects from those in gurdwaras. For example, they do not have the holy book, the *Guru Granth Sahib*, present at their meetings; nor do they distribute the *'parshad'* at the end of the prayers with the same reverence. Their membership cuts across caste groups. They have no centre of their own in Bradford. Their membership is small, about fifty families. They have been meeting regularly in a rented church hall for sat-sang (religious worship) for the last ten years at least. They have no locally elected leadership, and their guru resident in the Punjab appoints the person in charge of their organisational and religious affairs. *Radhaswamis* have some followings among people of European origin as well. It is interesting to note that currently an English lady, Mrs. Wood from London, is the appointed spiritual head of the UK *sangat.*

Naturally, the question arises what therefore binds the community together despite so much internal fragmentation. In my view, the prime sources from which the unity is derived include: the theoretical conception of Sikhism as a 'classless and casteless' way of life, its minority status (even in India), the history of perpetual persecution endured by Sikhs, and a constant threat to *Khalsa* identity. The popular presentation of the theoretical egalitarianism of Sikh beliefs, the history of Sikh struggles and heroic achievements, and the stories of historical and current persecutions, provides a psychological unity for all Sikhs. Such unity usually becomes evident, however temporarily, when they face external blows or threats to their collective religious identity. For example, in the mid eighties, the "Blue Star Operation" in Amritsar and the mass killing of Sikhs in Delhi pulled them together for a while.

CHAPTER 4

SIKHS AND THE ECONOMY

Immigrants contribute to the economy as workers in the labour market, providers of products or services, and as consumers. The level and the value of economic contribution of the immigrants who came to Britain in the middle of this century largely depended on the range and quality of skills they had to offer matched against the existing and potential demands such skills could satisfy. The prime contribution of South Asian workers, including Sikhs, to the local economies was in meeting the serious shortage of manual labour, particularly in textiles, engineering and public transport. Initially, as providers of products and services they were only meeting the particular needs of their own communities. They started penetrating beyond the narrow boundaries of their protected ethnic markets around the middle of the 1970s.

As consumers, initially they had a very high propensity to save and remit money to their families left behind in their home countries. Their traditional life styles were less expensive. Their traditional consumption habits and patterns started to change towards the end of the 1970s with the growing up of the second generation. The net economic contribution of a group depends on the balance between what it adds to the creation of wealth, pays in taxes and National Insurance on the one hand, and how much it draws out in welfare benefitson the other. Providing an estimate of this sort is a complex exercise and beyond the scope of this book. The socio-economic profile of Bradford Sikhs presented here should serve as an example of Sikh immigrants in Britain as a whole.

Male Employment

The story of the Sikhs' contribution to the British economy is not much different from that of other immigrant communities generally. Irrespective of their previous employment background, most of them were initially employed in the local industries with a shortage of labour, that is, in textile firms, engineering factories and public transport. In 1977 (Singh, 1978), 30 % of Sikh men worked in textile industry, 32 % in engineering, 12 % in construction, 10 % in transport and communication, and 12 % were in the distributive trades. Compared with the general local population they were highly over-represented in the above industries. In public administration, the distributive trades, insurance and finance, Sikhs were seriously under-represented.

Even in the 1970s, Sikhs in Bradford had a distinctly better socio-economic profile compared with other ethnic minority groups in the city. However, they had a lower social-economic position compared with Sikhs in the country as a whole. In Bradford, 6 out of 10 men worked in semi-skilled and unskilled manual jobs compared with only 4 out of 10 Sikhs in these categories nationally. This may be because of the different nature of the local labour market, and it could be due to the better educational and professional background of Sikhs in other parts of the country, particularly the areas closer to London, which tended to attract more Sikh immigrants of a middle class background. I have argued somewhere else (Singh, 1992) that the situation for the Sikhs in Bradford remains relatively unchanged: even now their socio-economic position differs from that of Sikhs in other parts of Britain.

Female Employment

The employment of Asian women in Britain is governed by economic, cultural and linguistic factors. Sikh women have few religious or cultural restrictions placed upon their working outside the home. Jobs requiring few skills and little knowledge of the English language were readily available. A keen desire to make good money quickly was a strong motivating force within Sikh families. Thus women were encouraged by their husbands to seek employment. Women's earnings facilitated buying and furnishing a house as well as providing a major boost to funds accumulated for investment in the Punjab. In 1977, in more than half of the Sikh families, the wife of the head of household was working full-time. Most of the women were in unskilled or semi-skilled jobs in the textile industry. Only a few worked on electrical engineering assembly jobs, as machinists in cloth manufacturing or as helpers in family businesses.

Factors Affecting the Pattern of Employment

The overall pattern of employment of Sikhs differed (and still does) from that of the general population of the city in some significant ways. For Sikh men or women there are no religious restrictions on the choice of jobs preventing them from spreading freely within the labour market. The economic ethics of Sikhism such as the belief in hard work, the dignity of labour, and the opposition to any kind of exploitation have implicitly influenced the position of Sikhs in the labour market.

Racial discrimination in employment kept Sikh men out of some areas of employment in the past, especially because of their beards and turbans. At the time of the 'turbans on the buses' dispute in Manchester in 1966, the typical attitude of the British public was neatly described in a lengthy editorial of the Telegraph & Argus (6 October 1966). It argued that if a Sikh felt strongly about the turban he should have remained in the community where his views were shared and furthermore the Sikh religious leadership should give individual Sikhs dispensation from the wearing of turbans where it did not accord with British practice. In Bradford, even as late as August 1980, Mother's Pride Bakery, in Gain Lane, suspended Balbinder Singh Boparai, a Sikh employee from work for growing a beard and wearing a turban. The city transport also enforced an unwritten ban on turbans for a very long time. The first turbaned Sikh conductor, Rajinder Singh was appointed in November 1968. (*Telegraph & Argus*, 14 November, 1968)

Other factors influencing the Sikh position in the labour market may include their lack of specific educational and professional qualifications, and the relevant experience required for some jobs. However, these reasons could apply only in some areas of the labour market where technical and professional qualifications were an essential requirement. Despite their full participation in the labour market in the early years of their settlement in the city, a significant number of educated Sikhs worked in lower level jobs totally inappropriate to their academic qualifications and previous employment experience. Therefore, most of them did not achieve their maximum potential for themselves.

Over the last fifteen years or so a significant number of Sikh children, more educationally qualified than their parents, have entered lucrative professions, such as accountancy, law, medicine, information technology, and pharmacy. The impact of this change on the overall industrial and occupational distribution of Sikhs in Bradford since the 1977 survey is difficult to quantify. However, general observations certainly suggest a significant improvement.

Most of the time, Sikhs have had a lower rate of unemployment compared with other South Asian communities in Britain. However, the unemployment rate, particularly among middle-aged Sikhs has gone up alongside structural changes in the local economy such as the fast decline in the textile and manufacturing industries. This has sharpened the socio-economic division within the Sikh community. There is a minority section of more affluent professional and successful businessmen at the one end and a significant minority group with reduced financial positions (and a gradually increasing dependence on state benefits) at the other end of the scale.

Sikh Businesses and Self-employment

In some sectors South Asians including Sikhs have created their own institutions and duplicated the provision of services. For example, a large number of grocery retail and wholesale outlets, clothing shops, car repairs, insurance, banks and travel services, restaurants, entertainment groups, ethnic presses, places of worship and community centres serve their own communities. For instance, the majority of Sikh men drink. British pubs offered them a favoured leisure time entertainment venue. However, their loud talking in Panjabi was always resented and many a time it resulted in their exclusion from some places. Panjabi customers wanted samosas and pakoras as snacks but pubs could offer only cockles and mussels. This difficulty was resolved in the acquisition of the Flying Dutchman, the Albion, the Victoria, the Lemon Tree and the Cemetery, five public houses on Leeds Road, by Sikh landlords. The Belle Vue and The Cartwright Hotel were added to the list later.

For years Sikh businesses operated in protected markets largely serving ethnic minority clients concentrated in the inner city areas. Since the major decline in textiles and large scale redundancies in public transport, many more Sikh men and women have gone into small family businesses, particularly running grocery and off-licence outlets, newspaper agencies and sub-post offices. However, during the last couple of decades the role and nature of these businesses have changed and their clientele has widened as a result. These businesses have spread more widely across the whole of the Bradford district and, therefore, serve the local population in general.

Those small-size Sikh businesses that started in almost invisible locations, serving their own community, have become visible and large. Now, they are big engineering manufacturers (Bradford Grinders in Mount Street, Ajax Minerva Ltd in Edderthorpe Street, and Sangha Metallurgy in Blanch Street). The story of Autoelectro in Leeds Road is a typical example of their development. Santokh Singh Bhogal, an inspector in the Marsden Radiators firm in Shipley, started Autoelectro in October 1966 as an alternators and car repair business in his home garage. Now it occupies massive premises and is run by his three sons, Tony, Nicky and Paul Bhogal. It employed 35 people in 1998 and had a turnover of over a million pounds. (*Telegraph & Argus*, 26 March 1998)

A number of electrical goods repair shops of the 1960s and the 1970s, for example, Amrik Electronics, SSTV, Empire Electrical Store, are now household names in the city. Empire Electrical Megastore in Ingleby Road began its life as an electrical retail shop in Leeds Road in 1984. It is a partnership of Showan brothers, Madan and Manohar, and Toor brothers, Jas and Amarjit. Currently it employs 150 people in its four outlets with an annual turnover of £30 million. (*Telegraph & Argus*, 12 January 1999)

In 1960s, Kohli & Company in Preston Street was one of the only two wholesale suppliers of South Asian foods in the North. At present, Bhatoa and Patel Grocery Warehouse serves a large number of retail businesses. Garment manufacturers and clothing firms, Dilbag Cloth House and Nirmal Rizai Mart are well-known exporters and importers in their areas of business. Travel agents, Zamindar Travel,

Sam Travel and Bharat Travel (now called Prime Travel) no longer serve only Asian clients but attract customers across the local communities. Bassra and Singh Solicitors and Bhatoa and Patel are established firms of legal services.

Sikh migrants to Britain included a section of highly skilled people, particularly from East African countries. They included builders, and plumbers and experienced vehicle repairers. Some of those who established themselves in their own trades in a very small way are now big names in the city. These include: Panesar Builders and Plumbing Merchants, Kundi & Sons Builders, Notey Builders, Raiyat Builders, Panesar Motors, Sagoo Motors, and BM Motors. A large number of full-time and part-time traders of various goods own and run stalls in local markets and many are self-employed builders and plumbers.

Bradford is now known as 'curry capital'. There are over two hundred Asian restaurants in Bradford and the number is growing every year. It is interesting to note that to date Rajput in Shipley is the only Sikh-owned restaurant in the city. An earlier one, the Punjabi Restaurant in Usher Street, closed within a year of its opening in 1995. At present most of these restaurants survive and flourish on the fast developing taste of the local white population for South Asian cuisine. Their South Asian clientele is small but increasing with the growing up of the second generation. With the growth of tourism to the district in the 1990s, the number of taxis in the city has increased. Whilst the Sikhs are known for their interest in transport and running taxis in all major cities of their settlement the world over, Bradford seems to be an exception. Here Pakistani Muslims run most of the taxis and Sikhs have shown little interest and initiative in this expanding sector of self-employment. It appears that Bradford Sikhs are not fully exploiting the economic opportunities that the developing tourist industry in the city is likely to create.

The external constraints imposed by racial discrimination and structural changes in the labour market have influenced the strategies chosen by Sikhs in the labour market. They appear to have gone for full assimilation. It is suggested that some members of ethnic minority communities are trying to use self-employment as a way to get around the problem of racial discrimination. However, the small number of South Asian manufacturers, including Sikh manufacturers, are not likely to provide jobs to all potential employment seekers. Thus the development of Sikh enterprises, although a significant phenomenon, is not a viable alternative area of employment for the majority. They themselves are quite conscious of this fact. There are some opportunities for a further increase in self-employment in small businesses, but most Sikh parents are encouraging their children to seek educational qualifications to go into the professional, business, financial and information technology sectors.

Sikh Consumers

In the 1960s and the 70s, the years of immigration, South Asian retail shops were like local 'corner shops' where news was exchanged, politics mentioned and gossip heard, but not any more. Now, for the Asian customer the social reasons for choosing these shops - such as staff speaking their community language, knowing the owner, or meeting friends - have lost their relevance. These shops are largely used for those items which are either not available in local supermarkets or are cheaper. South Asians indicate no ethnic commitment to buy from the shops owned by people of their own ethnic background. Because of their wider spatial dispersion in the city Sikhs, more than Pakistani and Bangladeshi Muslims and Gujarati Hindus, shop in supermarkets and other normal retail outlets, except for certain items, such as Indian dals, vegetables, chapatti flour, and jewellery. (Singh and Green, 1982) Sikhs use ethnic shops rationally and quite selectively, without any ethnic commitment.

The Sikhs' contribution to the local economy as consumers has varied over the different phases of their settlement. In the earlier years of immigration expenditure patterns were significantly influenced by factors such as a strong motivation to save, living in an all-male household, the myth of returning home, lack of time for leisure activities and the absence of family-related social expenditure. Even during the early period of their settlement as families most Sikhs had a reasonable standard of living. According to the 1977 survey, 60% of Sikh households had a car, 75% had a telephone in the house, 90% possessed a refrigerator and 50% owned a washing machine. Almost every Sikh household possessed a radio and a tape recorder and 75% of the households had carpets fitted in all rooms in the house. Possession of such facilities by working class households in the 1970s was normally associated with a middle class status. (Singh, 1980) During the last couple of decades there has been a gradual but significant decline in remittances to the Punjab. At the same time their general state of affluence is witnessed in their patterns of consumer expenditure, particularly at times of wedding celebrations and other social gatherings.

CHAPTER 5

GURDWARAS IN BRADFORD

The first gurdwara in Bradford - Garnet St.

At present Bradford has six gurdwaras. This chapter provides a brief history of each gurdwara and their role in the life of Bradford Sikhs. A profile of their management committees is contained in the Appendix.

Before Bradford had its own gurdwara, Sikhs in the city used to travel to Leeds on Sunday mornings to attend the services held in the gurdwara on Chapeltown Road. The first gurdwara in Bradford was established in an old carpet warehouse at 16-20 Garnett Street, off Leeds Road. The building was bought for £3500. After receiving the usual permission for the use of the building for religious services (19 September 1963) and £1000 for renovation of the building, it was opened for service on 29 March 1964.

The gurdwara was managed by the United Sikh Association, Bradford, led by Sardara Singh, president, and Gurmail Singh Sodhi, general secretary. On 6 September 1964, the United Sikh Association adopted its constitution. Two volunteers, Giani Sohan Singh and Piara Singh Nijhar normally conducted the weekly services. The annual religious celebrations were normally held in hired public halls, the Co-operative Hall in Thorton Road, Queens Hall in Morley Street and the St George's Hall, Hall Ings. At that time the Sikh population in Bradford was well under a thousand and predominantly male.

On 9 May 1965 the management committee of the United Sikh Association decided to build a new gurdwara and to start collecting money for the building. A plot of land was bought on Malvern Street / Ventor Street for this purpose. Before work on the new site was started Prospect Hall on Wakefield Road came on the market. The availability of this church hall raised the question whether the community should continue with its proposal for a new building on the purchased land or whether the church hall should be bought for only a fraction of the estimated cost of the new building. The management committee remained divided on this matter during 1969-70. A meeting of the Association on 21 February 1970 agreed that the existing management committee should continue to run the present premises. It further

Wakefield Rd.

agreed that those in favour of buying Prospect Hall on Wakefield Road and the group who insisted on constructing the new building on the Malvern Street site should form new separate committees to go head with their own projects. However, all three groups would have equal right to the assets of the Garnett Street gurdwara when it was sold. The conflict continued, the local council purchased the Garnett Street building for demolition, and the accounts of the Association were frozen.

Finally, a general body meeting of the United Sikh Association formally dissolved the Association on 27th September 1970 and merged it with the Bradford Sikh Association, managing the Guru Nanak Gurdwara, on Wakefield Road. After settling all the liabilities of the Association, Gurmail Singh Sodhi received a cheque for £5365.17 from the bank, which he handed over to the Bradford Sikh Association on 21 October 1973. The money was divided equally between the Guru Gobind Singh Gurdwara, Malvern Street, and the Guru Nanak Gurdwara.

At present, within about a one mile radius of the city centre, there are six gurdwaras: Guru Gobind Singh Sikh Temple in Malvern Street (renamed Gobind Marg in December 1998), off Leeds Road, Guru Nanak Sikh Temple on Wakefield Road, Ramgarhia Sikh Temple on Bolton Road, Amrit Parchar Dharmik Diwan Gurdwara in Harris Street, Guru Ravidas Bhavan in Brearton Street, and Singh Sabha Bradford Gurdwara, Grant Street.

Guru Gobind Singh Gurdwara is purpose-built, replacing the old Garnett Street Gurdwara, only a hundred yards away. The work on the new building, on the land bought for £2300, was started on 31 May 1970 and Edward Lyon, MP, laid its foundation stone. It was formally inaugurated on 12 March 1972 and the Indian High Commissioner, His Excellency, Apa V Pant, and the Lord Mayor of Bradford, local MPs and many other dignitries attended the ceremony. In 1975, a small building and a plot of land for car parking, adjoining the gurdwara building were bought for £75,000. Ten years later, in 1985, a new hall and some rooms were added to the gurdwara building. The extension was partly financed by a grant from Bradford Council's Community Programme. Currently (November 1999), some major alterations to the existing building are under construction.

There was no tradition of appointing a *Granthi*, honorary or paid, for conducting the services in the gurdwara. The work was carried out by volunteers, without any formal training as priests but with a knowledge of religious practices and experience of reading the *Guru Granth Sahib*. It was the first time in June 1976 that Gurchain Singh, a volunteer for years, was offered a paid appointment, which he declined. Gurcharan Singh was the first paid *granthi* appointed in August 1978 at a weekly honorarium of £40. A year later, in September 1979, Kulvinder Singh, an English-speaking young man with some training in conducting religious services and experience of teaching Panjabi to young children, was appointed on a slightly enhanced weekly salary of £50. Since then *granthi's* has been a paid position in the gurdwara. Currently there are two incumbents.

In the 1990s, all gurdwaras in the city felt the need to establish community centres for social activities, supported by, but separate from, gurdwaras. These centres would be able to cater for the serving of meat and alcoholic drinks at weddings and other social functions, strictly prohibited in gurdwaras. There was also a growing concern about the lack of younger Sikhs' participation in community activities at gurdwaras.

Leeds Road Gurdwara foundation stone

Sporting pursuits for boys, health courses, sewing classes and educational courses for women, together with leisure and entertainment facilities for elderly folks, were planned. With these intentions and with financial assistance from various sources, these centres came into existence. Success varies from centre to centre. The GGSG management committee established one such centre in May 1996, in the building of a private club bought for £174,000, in Herbert Street, off Leeds Road.

Guru Nanak Gurdwara is an old Methodist church, converted into a gurdwara. It was opened on 25 May 1970. The gurdwara was started by a splinter group of the United Sikh Association, Bradford, which had been managing the gurdwara in Garnett Street. The split occurred over the question of building a new gurdwara in Malvern Street or buying the Methodist Church on Wakefield Road. Those who favoured the low cost alternative of buying the Methodist Church (at £5000) to the construction of a new building at five times its £26,000 estimated cost, left the Association to form the trust for the GN Gurdwara. The original building was damaged by a fire (suspected arson and burglary) in March 1986 and its repairs cost the community nearly £100,000 to restore it to its original splendour. The gurdwara management committee, with generous grants from the Sports Council and the City Council, has established a large sports cum community centre, next door to the gurdwara building.

Amrit Parchar Dharmik Diwan is an organisation of *Amritdhari Sikhs*, founded by a small number of followers of the Sikh Sant, Baba Gian Singh Ji Johalanwale (Jalandhar). The organisation was initially based at the Guru Gobind Singh Gurdwara, Leeds Road. Due to their strong adherence to Sikh traditions they lost favour with a management committee dominated by *Sehajdhari Sikhs*. Kulvinder Singh, the appointed granthi was leading this group, and when his contract of services with the gurdwara was not renewed, the whole group drifted away. Initially they started their own separate weekly meetings in individual members' homes in turn until they bought the present premises.

It was originally a Zion Church, later converted into an Italian club. After a good deal of renovation the building was opened as a gurdwara on 24 October 1982.

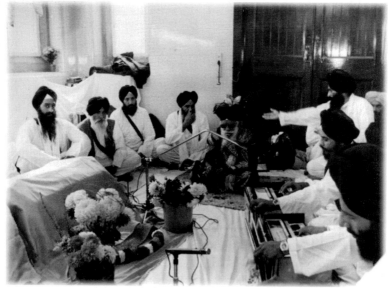

Harris St. - Amrit Parchar

The organisation has very close links with branches in some other cities in Britain. They attract visitors from other cities for special functions and on these occasions they hold *Amrit* (baptism) ceremonies. Unlike other gurdwaras in Bradford who elect their management committees annually or biannually, the management of this gurdwara is in the hands of a small number of members appointed with the consent of their spiritual leader in the Punjab.

Ramgharia Sikh Temple: Almost the same time as when the Amrit Parchar Dharmik Diwan group was organising itself as a separate entity from the Guru Gobind Singh Gurdwara, the Ramgarhia group was experiencing unease and tension in the Guru Nanak Gurdwara. The congregation in that gurdwara, although much smaller than that of the Leeds Road gurdwara, was dominated by members of the non-Jat castes, particularly the Ramgarhias. In the annual election for the management committee in 1979, the Ramgarhia group lost the election. It was the first and, perhaps, the last time to date that an election for a gurdwara's management in Bradford was contested on the basis of published manifestos by rival groups, which has become almost a common feature for gurdwaras in other cities in Britain in the 1990s. As a result, this group started holding their weekly services, initially on Saturday evenings, in a hired church hall in Rushton Street organised by their association, the Ramgarhia Board. The Board, a caste-based organisation, had been in existence since 1975. Victoria Hall on Bolton Road, an old dilapidated building, was bought by the Board in November 1980 and was opened as a gurdwara in April 1981. The Ramgarhia Board was finally dissolved in October 1979 and an elected committee took over the management of the gurdwara. This gurdwara has also established a community centre, not too far from its location, which is available to the public for social functions.

Wedding at Ramgharia Sikh Temple

Guru Ravidas Bhavan was opened on 6 June 1982. This is a big old three story building, previously cloth manufacturing premises, bought by Ravidas Sabha, an association of Ravidasias members of the Sikh community, that has existed in Bradford since the mid 1970s. The building was renovated to its present standard by the association through money raised from its members and a small grant from Bradford Council under its Community Programmes. Prior to the establishment of the Bhavan, the members of Ravidas Sabha used other gurdwaras to

45

celebrate the birth anniversaries (*gurpurbs*) of Guru Ravidas and for other social functions. But they frequently felt that they were being accorded an inferior status in the gurdwaras, generally dominated by members of the Jat caste. From 1977 they started celebrating Guru Ravidas Gurpurbs in the St. George's Hall until they established Guru Ravidas Bhavan in 1982.

Bradford Singh Sabha Gurdwara

was established by a splinter group of a younger group of Sikhs, mostly the members of the International Sikh Youth Movement (Bradford Branch) who were pushed out from their control of the Guru Gobind Singh Gurdwara in February, 1993. They were accused of changing the gurdwara constitution irregularly, mismanagement of gurdwara accounts, and failure to hand over the gurdwara records to the newly-formed committee. In July 1994, the group bought the building for £90,000 raised with donations and interest-free loans offered by 40-50 families. A trust was set up a month later to manage the building and the gurdwara was opened for worship in October 1994. Since then a further £91,000 has been spent on furnishing and extending the original premises. The main emphasis in the activities of the gurdwara is on *Amrit Sanchar* (baptising Sikhs) and teaching of Panjabi, *shabad keertan*, Sikh religion and *gatka* (Sikh marshal arts) to young people. Interestingly, in addition to the appointment of a board of trustees and a management committee,

Gatka team of young Sikhs from Bradford Singh Sabha Gurdwara

there is a board of five *jathedars*, whose function is to preside over and administer all religious celebrations and ceremonies strictly in accordance with the established Sikh religious practices.

Role of Gurdwaras

Gurdwaras are a unique and singularly the most important institution of the Sikh Diaspora. The first gurdwara in the UK was established in West London in 1911, at the initiative of some Sikh students and with a considerable donation from the Maharaja of Patiala, Bhupinder Singh. Soon after their settlement in Britain in the mid-fifties, Sikh migrants started buying old properties, many of them old church premises, and re-furbishing them into gurdwaras. At present there are well over 200 gurdwaras in Britain.

Most gurdwaras function as religious centres as well as social and political institutions of the local Sikh community. They provide a platform on which to discuss the entire spectrum of religious, social and political issues affecting the community. For local mainstream institutions and agencies these are the gateways and prime access routes into the community. Gurdwaras act as a "clearing house" for all sorts of information, news and views.

All gurdwaras hold regular religious services and provide similar ranges of facilities for social functions. For example, all Bradford gurdwaras provide exactly the same religious services. The only difference is in the stress each individual gurdwara may put on the observance of traditional religious practices. For instance, Amrit Parchar Dharmik Diwan follows the *Amritdhari* practices more rigidly and Guru Ravidas' writings are given more prominence in the Ravidas Bhavan. Although individual families may associate themselves more closely with a particular gurdwara for one reason or another, both in theory and practice they serve the community as a whole. Many people choose a gurdwara according to their convenience and the relative attractiveness of the service on particular occasions.

They offer arrangements for the solemnisation of social ceremonies relating to birth, child-naming, engagement, marriage and death. Most have arrangements for teaching Panjabi to young children. Panjabi classes are normally held at weekends. For example, in Bradford gurdwaras at present over 200 children attend these classes each week. Children are prepared for GCSE and "A"Level examinations. In most gurdwaras, the Sikh religion is not taught as part of the curriculum in these classes. If children learn anything about Sikhism, Sikh history or Punjabi culture, it is all incidental. Therefore, these classes make a very limited contribution to the development of Sikh identity amongst the second generation of Sikhs. However, the demand for the teaching of Panjabi by the gurdwaras is likely to continue even when many local education authorities in Britain have made some provision for its teaching in mainstream schools with a concentration of Sikh children. Most gurdwaras may even have small libraries. Generally, their library stocks contain a selection of books on the Sikh religion and history, mostly in Panjabi, whilst the bulk of books are expected to be popular Panjabi fiction.

The gurdwaras are extremely useful in providing a social environment for women and elderly Sikhs. For some the time spent in gurdwaras in the company of others is the only entertainment possible outside the home. It helps them to avoid feelings of loneliness and boredom. There are many small routine jobs in a gurdwara, such as cleaning, cooking and serving food, serving *Karah Parshad*, which are normally done by women and elderly people. Doing these jobs is not simply satisfying but provides a feeling of being wanted by, and a service to, their community.

Management of Gurdwaras

Management committees, elected or appointed by the formally enrolled memberships of local *sangats*, run most gurdwaras. The committees are elected or appointed annually or bi-annually according to the procedures laid down in the written constitution of the particular gurdwara, in theory at least. However, the British experience suggests that the approved constitutions have been violated more often than followed. Generally, an election board set up by the outgoing committee, attempts to form a new committee from the list of nominations received or it selects individuals to serve on the committee. Since the mid eighties, it is noticeable how fiercely contested the elections in many gurdwaras in Britain have become, with manifestos of different contesting groups, including the photographs of candidates, published in national Panjabi weeklies.

Unlike this national trend, gurdwaras in Bradford, so far, have been an exception. The only example of an election contested in this manner in Bradford, which the author can recall, is that of the 1979 elections of Guru Nanak Gurdwara, which two groups contested on the basis of their published manifestos. However, this does not signify the absence of fierce internal manoeuvring by the different factions in the sangat to obtain a majority position in the management committees of local gurdwaras. For example, Ramgarhia Sikhs had the major influence on the management of Guru Nanak Gurdwara until 1979. The management committee of Guru Gobind Singh Gurdwara has always been dominated by Jat Sikhs. Guru Ravidas Bhavan and Ramgarhia Gurdwara committees are entirely composed of Ravidasias and Ramgarhias, respectively. Officials appointed from a small discrete group in each gurdwara manage Amrit Parchar Dharmik Diwan Gurdwara and the Singh Sabha Gurdwara. The sangat has no role in these appointments.

The most serious common difficulty in the management of gurdwaras arises from the conflict between the traditional overarching religious authority of the *sangat* and the procedures created through formally adopted consitutions. At times decisions taken by elected representatives are reversed or rescinded by the *sangat*. The classic example in Bradford was an open, prolonged conflict between the *sangat*, the trustees and the elected management committee of the gurdwara in Garnet Street, about the decision to build Guru Gobind Singh Gurdwara on its present site. Many cases of internal conflicts within the management committees of gurdwaras in Britain, sometimes resulting in court cases, have been a direct consequence of this contradiction between the powers of the *sangat* and formal constitutions. The number of such cases over the years has increased. The resolution of most cases results in prolonged expensive court cases or some serious intervention by the Charities Commission.

Sikhism provides, in theory, every Sikh an equal right to express his or her views freely in the sangat. The will of the *sangat* is considered to be supreme. Nevertheless, the inherent weakness of taking a decision in the *sangat* is that it reflects the views and wishes of a small number of articulate members only. Most ordinary members remain silent, either to avoid a serious public debate which might violate the religious sanctity of gurdwara or because they lack the confidence and skills required to articulate their views in large gatherings. Voting, open or secret, a fundamental procedure in the resolution of contested matters in organisations, is uncommon in the Sangat, as the *sangat* is believed to be a sacred collectivity of people. Thus, even a silent majority against a proposal may not be able to influence the decision at all. Therefore, many *sangat* decisions generally portrayed as unanimous, in reality, are minority decisions. Furthermore, they are based more often on sentiment and emotion, rather than on reason and consensus of opinion.

The officials of gurdwara management committees exercise significant influence on affairs within the community and its relationship with outside bodies and other communities. Most gurdwaras have a *granthi* (or *granthis*), an appointed priest. He (universally a man) is normally responsible for conducting routine religious services, organising religious and social events, teaching Panjabi classes and taking general care of the gurdwara. Not all *granthis* are professionally trained. Most of them may simply have an ability to read the *Guru Granth Sahib*, an understanding and knowledge of religious and social customs, and an ability to organise and conduct services. Their sphere of activities and influence is normally confined to the gurdwaras. They have little involvement with the wider community and its agencies. Ironically, despite their important and essential services to the community, they enjoy only low esteem for their profession.

All gurdwaras in the Sikh Diaspora are maintained from the regular income received from individual offerings. These donations can be substantial. For example, the fact that a small Sikh community of less than seven thousand people in Bradford can maintain six large places of worship shows the generosity of the Sikhs towards religious contributions. On many occasions money has been collected by public appeals, door to door collections and through offers of interest-free loans from individuals, specifically for furnishing, buying or extending gurdwara buildings.

Over the last twenty years the religious activity within the Sikh Diaspora has significantly increased. The present author's observations in Canada, Kenya, USA, Fiji, New Zealand, Australia and Singapore confirm that the story of the development of gurdwaras in Bradford is consistent with gurdwaras in other cities in Britain and the Diaspora.

During the last two decades the number of gurdwaras in each locality of Sikh concentration has increased. But the number has not risen purely to meet the additional demand of a growing community. Many have been set up as a direct result of conflict between different factions in management committees. Conflicts are based on intense competition for group influence and individual leadership within the community. In many instances, a split in the management committee or loss of control leads to the setting up of a new gurdwara by the losing group. A significant number of gurdwaras have been established by famous Sikh saints from the Punjab for their own devotees. The caste divisions have also led to the establishment of separate gurdwaras, particularly in the case of *Ramgarhias, Ravidasias* and *Bhatras*. Most gurdwaras have become a major source of internal tension and conflict within the community. The atmosphere in gurdwaras has generally become religiously intense and politically charged. Currently, they are attracting an increased number of people to their services.

Attendance at Gurdwaras

Most gurdwaras hold their regular weekly services on Sunday mornings. However, with the appointment of paid *granthis* in gurdwaras, the buildings are generally open for worship throughout the week. Over the years attendance at gurdwaras has increased for a variety of reasons. On special celebrations attendance may reach several hundred people.

Firstly, there is a general increase in the Sikh population in most cities and there is little decline in their interest in religion. Most Sikhs are religious-minded, even if many do not display any serious commitment to regular worship. The occasional visit to a gurdwara provides consolation and some comfort about having done their duty to remember God. This is particularly so in the case of most women.

Secondly, it is Sikh women, old or young, who are the prime initiators and motivators within families to encourage children and male members to visit gurdwaras.

Why women should be more inclined to visit a gurdwara than their menfolks, is a difficult fact to explain. However, in Britain their stronger interest in religion and commitment to attend gurdwaras may be due to a number of reasons.

(a) They have few opportunities and places outside home where they can freely meet other women without any concerns being expressed by the family or suspicions being raised. This is particularly so with women from a non-professional background who may have limited knowledge of English and mainstream culture or who come from very traditional and conservative families.

(b) Women with serious domestic or health problems turn to religion for comfort and solace, more often than ego-ridden men.

(c) The work (*sewa*) in the community kitchen (*langar*) and the cleaning of gurdwara premises are considered valuable and gratifying tasks, and a service to the community. This is particularly so, given the current situation that they have little opportunity to play a significant role in the leadership and management of gurdwaras.

(d) The informal nature of the gurdwara congregation allows women to view and discuss the latest fashion in Punjabi garments and jewellery, to catch up with the information and gossip about weddings, births, deaths in different families as well as about 'unmentionable' divorces, affairs and run-away girls.

Thirdly, gurdwaras have started celebrating more and more religious functions particularly since the 1984 Blue Star Operation in Amritsar and the subsequent developments in the Punjab. These events have generated an enormous rejuvenation of religious feelings amongst Sikhs in Britain and elsewhere and a renewed attempt by many to adopt the Khalsa identity. It is also due to the fact that sants, *keertani jathas* and *ragi-dhadi jathas* from India have started coming to Britain in increased numbers. They generally attract good audiences due to their professional performances.

Fourthly, the size of gatherings in gurdwaras is very much inflated on social functions such as weddings; *akhand-paths* and langars organised by individual families to which their relatives and friends are specifically invited. Over the years, the holding of such social celebrations in gurdwaras rather than in family homes as was the tradition, have increased manifold. Hardly a weekend passes without such a celebration in almost every one of the local gurdwaras.

Fifthly, gurdwaras are also the centre stage of community politics. The internal politics of the gurdwara management committees attract wide interest within the local Sikh community (*sangat*s). Most attendees enjoy the infights for leadership and controlling power. This is closer to their everyday life (like village politics) than the activities of mainstream political organisations.

Sixthly, as the proportion of people in the retirement group increases and the number of older people out of work becomes bigger, they find more leisure time on their hands, particularly those without major family and social commitments and a lack of direction in life. They congregate in gurdwaras for socialisation even if they have no strong religious commitments. Gurdwaras offer them company, unrestricted comfortable space and even free food (on most days now).

Gurdwaras are the nerve centres of local Sikh communities. However vital their religious services may be to the Sikh community, they do not appear to have taken on seriously the enhanced role they could play in dealing with the issues concerning the social well-being of the Sikh community and its rightful place in mainstream society. The harsh reality is that, at present, many gurdwara leaders do not generally possess adequate communication skills, the experience, confidence and vision to deal with the institutions of the wider society. Their leadership seems to be preoccupied with gaining and maintaining control of individual gurdwaras and with the politics of the Punjab.

CHAPTER 6

COMMUNITY DEVELOPMENT, ORGANISATIONS AND LEADERSHIP

In the early years of immigration there was no Sikh community (or communities) in Britain, as we know it today. There were large groups of Sikh migrants from the Punjab settled in different cities. The individuals related to each other on the basis of family connections or as co-villagers. As the immigration was from a very compact area in the Punjab there was also a close social affinity among them. On arrival in Britain, most of them experienced similar problems in finding work and living accommodation, faced white prejudice and discrimination and common difficulties in dealing with the official agencies. They all missed their home culture, its support systems and the flavour of home politics. As the size of local groups increased and with family consolidation, the need for extending the existing networks became apparent. More formal organisations were needed to meet their growing social, welfare and leisure needs.

The first such Sikh organisations to come into being were related to the establishment and management of gurdwaras. Although, as described earlier, in addition to their role as religious institutions gurdwaras do meet a wide variety of the social, welfare, and political needs of Sikhs, yet they can act only within certain religious limitations. The role of earlier community organisations was very much to provide what the gurdwaras could not do effectively or could not do at all. Thus, the aims and objectives of various organisations that emerged in the 1950s and 60s were fairly general. These included social welfare, the provision of guidance and help to members in dealing with official agencies, the development of contacts with the local white community, the arrangement of recreational activities such as poetry readings and the showing of Indian movies, the celebration of national events and religious festivals. Only the Indian Workers' Association, Great Britain, had the fight against white prejudice and discrimination as an explicit objective.

Bradford Sikh Community Organisations

As in other cities, some of the groups organised in Bradford by the local Sikhs were fairly small and short lived, thus having a minimal effect on the community, whereas others involved the community at large and have served it well.

Indian Association (Bradford)

The presence of the Indian Association in the city was first reported in the Telegraph & Argus (16 June1964) when its members met in the St George's Hall on 7 June, 1964 to commemorate the death of Pandit Jawahar Lal Nehru, Prime Minister of India. At that time, Sikhs in the city did not have any separate organisation of their own. The officers of the association included one Sikh, Mr B S Bassi as vice president. Other officials, Mr S Malik (secretary), Mr Sunder (President), and Mr S Patel (treasurer), were all Hindus. The Association, based at 64 Victoria Street, acquired 17 Drewton Street as its new premises in August. (Telegraph & Argus, 12 August 1964) In December the tenancy of the Indian Association's Drewton Street premises was transferred to the Nehru Memorial Club, a non-political international social club set up by Mr Malik. He was granted a licence to sell liquor on the premises. Lady Bomanji officially opened the club and the venture had the blessings of theIndian High Commission in London. With the establishment of a local branch of the Indian Workers' Association (Great Britain), Sikhs in the city gradually stoppedparticipating in its activities.

The Indian Workers' Association, Great Britain (IWA, GB)

IWA (GB) is perhaps one of the oldest Indian organisations in Britain. It was established in 1938 in Coventry by a handful of Indian workers. It remained dormant for a long period. It was relaunched in 1953 and by 1957 had branches in most cities of Indian settlement. It aimed to organise Indian immigrants for participation in political activities. (Hiro1991, James 1974, John 1969 and Josephides 1991). From the beginning the leadership of the local IWA consisted of two major groups: moderate entrepreneurs and political radicals. Sikhs, who had been active supporters of one or other factions of the Communist Party of India, always dominated it. For most of the time, there had been two rival IWA's in Britain, reflecting the two factions of the Communist Party of India.

In principle the IWA is a non-religious organisation, however for practical and tactical reasons, the local IWAs have tried to keep in close contact with the gurdwaras. The gurdwaras provide an easy contact point with the Sikh community from which IWAs have always recruited their membership. Gurdwaras with Jat-Sikhs' predominance supported IWA more actively as Jats had been the main supporters of the Communist Party in the Punjab.

Photograph by kind permission of the Telegraph & Argus, Bradford

Telegraph and Argus, Monday, March 24, 1969   11

Some of the contingent which left Bradford yesterday for the Birmingham rally.

Since the early sixties the IWA (GB) has had a branch in Bradford. Bradford gurdwaras have generously supported IWA physically and financially in organising campaigns and demonstrations against the National Front and other right wing organisations. Gurdwaras also provide big gatherings for dissemination of information and the exchange of views. Despite the general support for the IWA's anti-racism and anti-discrimination policies, there is not much appreciation of their pre-occupation with Indian politics.

At present there are two IWAs in Bradford: one is the local branch of IWA (GB) and the other is IWA (Marxist-Leninist). There is little evidence to suggest any

Migrant law protest march

A 30-strong Indian contingent from Bradford left the city yesterday to join 4,000 of their fellows in a protest march to Birmingham against tightening of immigration laws.

Fourteen branches of the Indian Workers' Association of Great Britain throughout the country converged on Birmingham, marched through the city centre and attended a meeting later at Birmingham town hall.

Before leaving Bradford, the association's national president, Mr. Gurnam Singh, said: "We are demonstrating against the Indian Government as much as the British. The Indian Government attitude is that of a collaborator with the British Government. Our Prime Minister, instead of condemning racialism and British policies, keeps mum and remains indifferent towards the plight of the Indians living here."

56

significant influence of either of the two IWAs' on the internal affairs of the Sikh community in Bradford

The IWA (M-L), under the leadership of Jagtar Singh Sahota and Harbhajan Singh Dhesi, won some credibility in the late 1970s by playing an effective leading role in two local issues concerning the South Asian community. It mobilised strong parental opposition to the racially discriminatory 'bussing policy' of the local Educational Services Committee. The policy was investigated by the Commission for Racial Equality and eventually scrapped. It also launched a strong protest against racial discrimination in the recruitment and promotion practices of the West Yorkshire Passenger Transport Executive, the allegation which resulted in a successful formal investigation by the Commission for Racial Equality. In 1980 the Association claimed a membership of about three hundred but presently its membership is limited to a handful of activists. Its present activities are confined to running a Day Centre on Leeds Road for older people, the capital and running costs of which are provided through a grant under the Community Programmes of Bradford Council.

The IWA (GB), under the leadership of Gurnam Singh Sanghera, was a very active organisation in the sixties but became almost dormant in the seventies. At present, with the efforts of a small number of active officials it runs a community centre in a building on Wakefield Road, bought in 1986 through a grant provided by Bradford Council under its Community Programmes. The centre provides regular sewing classes for women, Panjabi classes and recreational facilities for the young, social and entertainment facilities for elderly members. Officials provide free advice to members on welfare matters. The Association is no longer affiliated to the national parent body. It has shifted its focus from political to purely social activities and individual advice.

Shromini Akali Dal (SAD)

SAD is a national organisation of the Sikhs in Britain. The organisation is modelled on the constitution of Shromini Akali Dal Amristar, the main Sikh political party in the Punjab. The link is not only ideological, as the functioning of the SAD in Britain is deeply influenced and guided by the parent body in Punjab. The leaders of the

SAD look for direction and even intervention from Amritsar at times of crisis within the party in Britain. Whenever there has been a split or change in the leadership of SAD in Amritsar, a similar change has occurred in the SAD in Britain. Within the Sikh community there has always been a good deal of confusion about the real SAD, as a number of factions have always existed. All sections of the SAD have largely been concerned with the politics of its parent body and have treated the problems of Sikhs in Britain as of secondary importance. SAD's major success has been its stance upon the turban issue in Britain. The focus of its activities has always been Birmingham in the Midlands and Southall in the London area.

A branch of the SAD was opened in Bradford in 1969 but it did not last more than a year. A fresh attempt was made to revive the local branch in 1979, but without much success. However, the local gurdwaras have given the SAD very generous support in its activities with regard to the problems of Sikhs in Britain. The issue of turbans on buses in Wolverhampton, Manchester and Leeds and 'crash helmet' legislation are examples of issues over which the SAD and the gurdwaras have worked together.

Ramgharia Board

Twenty-four *Ramgarhia* Sikhs from Bradford and Halifax formed the Ramgarhia Board in September 1975. Its constitution was formally adopted in a meeting on 13 March 1976 and the membership continued to increase. Its membership and activities were limited to *Ramgarhia* Sikhs only. The local Board was affiliated to the national Ramgarhia Board, as are all the *Ramgarhia* gurdwaras and local boards in Britain. The Board was a fairly inactive organisation until 1978 when a proposals to establish a separate gurdwara for the *Ramgarhia* community was discussed in its meetings. *Ramgarhias* had a strong representation in the management committee of Guru Nanak Gurdwara, Wakefield Road. In 1978, a serious split occurred in the gurdwara management committee and *Ramgarhias* lost the overall majority. It was a caste-based split, which caused strong feelings of animosity between *Ramgarhia* Sikhs, particularly those from East Africa and Jat-Sikhs from the sub-continent. Situations of a similar nature had also been observed in

Southall (Peggie, 1979), Birmingham and some other cities, where *Ramgarhias* had already established their separate gurdwaras.

As a consequence of the split, the Board became active and in October 1979 it started holding weekly meetings for religious worship in St. Margaret's Church Hall at Upper Rushton Road, Thornbury. In November 1980, the Board bought Victoria Hall at Bolton Road and opened it as the *Ramgarhia* Gurdwara, on 18 April 1981. After that the Boards' separate entity was finished and it basically merged with the new management of the gurdwara.

The Bradford Educational and Cultural Association of Sikhs (BECAS)
Bradford Sikh Parents' Association (BSPA)

The BSPA was formed by a small number of active young educated parents in 1981. It was formed to monitor the implications for Sikh children of changes in the Local Education Authority's policy about the education of ethnic minority children. From the mid-seventies the education of immigrant children became a controversial issue in Bradford. The IWA had fought against the discriminatory policies of medical testing of immigrant children prior to school admissions. Bussing of Asian children away from neighbourhood schools to other schools with the twin objectives of maintaining some racial balance in local schools, and facilitating the learning of English and other aspects of local cultures by Asian children, was bitterly resented and contested. At the same time the Muslim Parents' Association was voicing its serious resentment over some aspects of school life, e.g., the physical education outfit, school uniform for girls, mixed swimming and games, the Christian ethos of schools, and sex education.

In response to these concerns, the Local Education Authority introduced a number of changes in its policies for the education of South Asian children in the beginning of the eighties including the phasing out of the 'bussing policy'. Most of the Sikhs viewed these new developments as meeting only the particular concerns of Muslims, the numerically dominant community amongst the ethnic minority groups in the city. They felt the danger of their own particular needs relating to the provision for the teaching of Punjabi and Sikh religious education in schools being overlooked or marginalised. Despite such concerns the gurdwaras made very little input into the public debate about changes in educational policies. Therefore, the Sikh Parents' Association made its prime objective to raise the voice of their community on educational matters generally, and in particular their concerns about the education of Sikh children in the city.

Sikh Parents' Association conference held at Bradford

Since its formation, despite its small size, the Association has enjoyed the full support of other Sikh organisations in its activities. The Association earned recognition from the LEA for its contributions towards the development and implementation of its multi-cultural education policy. The Association followed a successful programme of organising Asian music classes for the young, annual poetry reading symposia, and holding educational seminars and conferences. It struggled for a number of years to obtain a grant for establishing a large community centre for Sikhs, but abandoned its efforts in 1993 and successfully supported the building of a community and sports hall by the Guru Nanak Gurdwara, Wakefield Road. A small group of founder members, Mohan Singh, Sukhdev Singh, Mohinder Singh Chana, Harjap Singh Pooni, Nirmal Singh, Joginder Singh Pabial, Balbir Singh, Mohinder Singh Khinda, Joga Singh, Kuldip Singh, Ramindar Singh and Hardev Singh Sidhu have served this association consistently in various capacities.

Reflecting on the nature of its activities over the past years and its changed role in the community, the Association decided to amend its constitution and adopt a new name. The new organisation was launched in November 1997, under the name: The Bradford Educational and Cultural Association of Sikhs. At present, Mohinder Singh Khinda is Chairman and Nirbhai Singh Bhandal is General Secretary.

Sikh Parents' Association conference held at Bradford College

Federation of Bradford Sikh Organisations (FBSO)

The FBSO came into being as a consequence of a very eventful period in the early eighties for the Sikhs in Bradford. As discussed earlier the number of gurdwaras increased from two to five largely as a result of internal divisions within the community. The growth in internal factionalism increased the number of leaders and intensified the rivalries and competition for leadership.

The attack on the Golden Temple, Amritsar, by the Indian Army in June 1984, the assassination of the Indian Prime Minister, Mrs Indira Gandhi, in October 1984, followed by the mass killing of Sikhs in Delhi and some other Indian cities roused the feelings of Sikhs all over the world. Following these events, the rise of militancy among the Sikhs, particularly among Sikh youth in the Punjab, impacted upon the image of Sikhs all over the world. The media projected the Sikhs as militants, terrorists and, basically, as criminals. Sikh communities all over the world felt deeply

61

concerned about correcting this biased and damaging image.

Photograph by kind permission of the Telegraph & Argus, Bradford

Burning of the effigy of Indira Gandhi

All Bradford Sikh organisations expressed similar concerns. But there was no central body to represent the common Sikh view on these developments. To resolve this difficulty the local branch of the newly formed International Sikh Youth Federation called a meeting of all Sikh organisations. The meeting agreed to set up an umbrella organisation. An ad hoc committee of representatives from all organisations was formed in June 1984 to act as the Federation of Bradford Sikh Organisations (FBSO). The FBSO was formally constituted a year later and adopted a much wider role in its constitution. Its objectives include: to act as a representative body of all local Sikh organisations; to work towards raising the status of the Sikh community; to counteract anti-Sikh forces; and to promote Sikhism, in addition to dealing with the crisis situation arising from current events.

The establishment of the FBSO was not an isolated development in the South Asian community in the city. The Muslims and Hindus had already established the Bradford Council of Mosques and the Hindu Vishwa Parishad, respectively. The FBSO was successful in maintaining good harmonious relations between Hindus and Sikhs in the city in the very stressful and strained circumstances of the Punjab Crisis, and established a close relationship with the Bradford Council of Mosques, other local community organisations and Bradford Council. Within the Sikh community itself it brought about greater unity. Unlike some other cities in Britain, the relations between the established gurdwara-based traditional leadership (relatively older in age) and the members of the new youth movements emerging all over Britain, has remained more cordial and smooth through the mediation of the FBSO. The following honorary officers served the organisation during its active life of almost ten years:

Year	Chairman	Secretary
1984/85	Ramindar Singh	Harjinder Singh Atwal
1985/87	Ramindar Singh	Sarwant Singh Dosanjh
1987/89	Manjit Singh Cheema	Mohinder Singh Chana
1989/91	Narinder Singh	Govinder Singh Dhaliwal
1991/92	Pavitar Singh	Rajinder Singh Panesar
1992/93	Balbir Singh	Harjap Singh Pooni
1993	Mewa Singh Bussan	Rajinder Singh Panesar

The organisation suddenly waned after 1993 and no attempt has been made to revive it. Its demise has made it difficult for Sikh organisations in the city to provide a common view on any matters or to co-ordinate activities such as the annual Vaisakhi procession. Currently (November 1999) fresh attempts are being made to revive it.

International Sikh Youth Federation (ISYF)

The ISYF was set up in Britain in September 1984 following the events in Amritsar in June 1984. The Federation was dedicated to the establishment of Khalistan, an independent Sikh state in India. It enjoyed a good deal of support from most gurdwaras in Britain. It was particularly active in the Midlands and London areas. The Federation effectively took control of a number of gurdwaras in Britain and maintained close links with parallel organisations in India, Canada and the USA. Over the years, internal factionalism has basically destroyed the movement in Britain. A branch of the ISYF was set up in 1984 in Bradford. The local branch, with a membership of about thirty people, was based at the Guru Gobind Singh Gurdwara on Leeds Road. Its local activities were very much confined to this gurdwara and to the annual celebration of the *Vaisakhi* festival. The members of the local Federation, who had virtually managed the Leeds Road gurdwara for a few years lost control in 1993. As a consequence they set up a separate Bradford Singh Sabha gurdwara. The organisation suffered from the same problem of internal divisions as its national body and at present its activities are limited to the running of the gurdwara.

Yorkshire Sikh Forum

A few well-known Sikh businessmen and professionals from Bradford, Leeds and Huddersfield set up the Yorkshire Sikh Forum in 1992. At its official launch on 30 November 1994, the secretary of the Forum, Harjap Singh Pooni, described its aim "to improve the economic, educational, social and cultural development of the Sikh community in Yorkshire." He emphasised its non-political and non-religious approach in representing the Sikh community. Nirmal Singh Sekhon MBE, Harjap Singh Pooni and Joginder Singh Pabial from Bradford have held various key positions in the management committee of the forum. So far, the Forum has remained a close group of a few individuals. Its selective membership has given the forum an elitist image. However, it appears to have established good contacts with officials in high positions in local and national governmental agencies in its short life.

Sikh Leadership

The specific interests and personalities of individual leaders or small groups dominate the activities of most Sikh organisations. The experience in Bradford suggests that, with the exception of gurdwaras, most Sikh organisations appear to have only weak independent corporate identities of their own. They lack widely shared objectives to keep their members united. Internal factionalism gives birth to a new organisation rather than a change in leadership. Within organisations the tradition of discussing matters dispassionately and thrashing out problems with reason has not developed. Winning an argument is considered a 'personal victory' and losing an argument a 'personal defeat'. Whenever there is a threat to the established leadership, even general criticism ends up in personal enmity and character assassination. In such a situation, many sensible members more often choose to remain silent to avoid being controversial. For individual leaders it is not possible to maintain their position of leadership on the strength of their personal merits and contributions to the work of the organisation. They must have a following of their caste, village group and relatives behind them. In this respect the Sikh leadership follows the distinctive traditional style of its counterpart in the Punjab.

The drive for self-advancement is very strong among Sikhs. In the early years of immigration the success of a migrant was measured in his ability to add to the family wealth in the Punjab. Little regard was paid to his standard of life and social status in Britain. Not many individuals thus aspired after leadership of the community in Britain. Those who played leading roles in the organisation of gurdwaras did so as a religious duty or 'service' to the community, rather than to gain 'leadership' of the community. The only reward was in the form of recognition of their services and respect within the Sikh community itself.

With the growing size of the community, the need to establish formal contacts with local agencies and their leadership became essential at the community level. In response to this need, migrants of professional middle class backgrounds formed some organisations with cultural, welfare and advice functions. They could speak English, had contacts with the local community, and had some political interests. These individuals were accepted automatically as the leaders of the community. An ordinary migrant, however, was still too busy working and earning money. He was indifferent to the position of these self-styled leaders and their newly created organisations. The concept of voluntary advisory and welfare organisations and their role as pressure groups was totally alien to most migrants from the rural areas of Punjab. Some of them joined the organisations because they knew the leader as a relative, friend or a fellow villager. No questions were asked and no interest was taken in the working of the organisation, and the leaders remained stable and free to act in their own way.

The situation is very different today. People have become conscious of their status within the community here. One way of enhancing social status within their own community is to obtain an official position within an ethnic organisation, because this normally provides recognition in the wider community too. Thus the number of potential candidates for offices in these organisations has increased greatly. Those aspiring to enter local politics and mainstream institutions recognise the need to create a power base within their own community. A strong and recognised position in their own community enhances their authority and enables them to negotiate with outsiders more firmly.

The traditional leaders of the community are relatively more successful in their personal achievements. They hold good jobs or own small businesses, live in good houses and enjoy a good standard of living. Examining carefully the cases of Sikh leaders in Bradford one would conclude that their personal achievements are due to factors such as higher educational qualifications, enterprising efforts, occupational mobility, hard work and the length of their stays in this country. Some members of the community tend to relate the personal success of these leaders to the positions they have held or hold within Sikh or other ethnic organisations

It is natural that wider contacts within the community at large are helpful to any individual to establish in new circumstances, but one could grossly overstate the gains which ethnic minority leaders have made because of their official positions in community organisations. However, their relative prosperity has developed feelings of keen competition for recognition and status within the community and has led to a certain amount of jealousy as well.

It should also be noted here that, in spite of women's active participation in gurdwaras and the activities of other community organisations, they are conspicuously absent from the leadership of Sikh organisations. Despite the liberal traditions of Sikhism and its emphasis on equal status for women in every aspect of life, Sikh organisations do not seem to encourage women to occupy leadership roles in their management committees. With traditional modesty, Sikh women are still reluctant to challenge male authority in the public domain. Furthermore, the general ethos of management committee meetings is not conducive for those women who may aspire to join the official ranks to make an effective contribution. They are likely to feel frustration and isolation because of the domineering attitude of most male members. In most Sikh families the change in the role and status of women at home is accepted by male members but women are not encouraged to accept offices in community organisations. Male members of the family are very protective of their women's izzat (honour). Any disrespectful remarks by an outsider may result in trouble involving the whole family. Community leaders appear to be aware of the issue of women's absence from management positions and at times talk about their good intentions to involve women in leadership roles, however they are not succeeding in altering the current unsatisfactory situation.

As the Sikh community is well established now and as most Sikhs are familiar with the functioning of mainstream institutions, the need for them to establish separate social and welfare type organisations has become less urgent. The gurdwara leadership is gradually narrowing its field of activities and confining itself more and more to the religious affairs of the community. They seem to be no longer interested in representing the community in all situations as they used to do previously. Other organisations are trying to adopt specific roles but they recognise the importance of keeping close links with local gurdwaras. An interesting development appears to be the declining interest of young Sikhs in the field of race and community relations. Also Bradford Sikhs seem to be slow in producing leaders with strong political ambitions.

CHAPTER 7

TRANSFORMATIONS IN SIKH IDENTITY

The reason why most of the pioneer Sikh immigrants to Britain stopped wearing turbans was, perhaps, to avoid becoming targets for unwanted attention. Up to the end of 1950 most of them were clean-shaven; despite the fact that they wore turbans and kept beards before emigration. Their decision to dispense with the most visible symbols of Sikh appearance has the following practical and philosophical explanations.

- Some dispensed with their beards and turbans purely for pragmatic reasons, such as the lack of time for tying turbans and pressing beards before going to work and the lack of adequate bathing and washing facilities in their living accommodation.

- The overt discrimination in employment against turbaned Sikhs in Britain was the most significant reason behind their changed appearance. Their clean-shaven patrons or relatives advised the new arrivals that to obtain employment quickly they would have to follow their example. Desperate to earn an immediate income, the newcomers found it difficult to go against the authentic-sounding advice of those they were relying upon for help in finding accommodation, employment as well as cash for their short-term survival.

- The change from being observing Sikhs to clean-shaven Sikhs did not invoke any deep feelings of guilt in the minds of many, as it appeared to be a mass phenomenon and not an isolated act of individual deviance.

- Most of them were keen to appease their local white hosts' feelings of insecurity and resentment about the fast-growing presence of alien cultures in the inner cities of industrial Britain.

- Educated migrants even aspired to seek social acceptance by the host community through altering their distinctive Sikh appearance. For them the motivation to change was not just the economic expediency of gaining secure employment. They were equally anxious to obtain some sort of social status within the larger society by adopting a western outlook. This was also perceived by many as more progressive and civilised than their own traditional life styles.

- A significant section of the Sikh population in India is called *Sehajdharis*. They are not regarded as full members of the *Khalsa Panth* as they do not observe the five prescribed symbols. However, they are accepted as equal members of the Sikh *sangat*. Newly clean-shaven Sikhs in Britain legitimised their religious deviance in terms of the *Sehajhdhari* tradition.

- Many Sikh immigrants belonged to the lower rural working classes in the Punjab. In these groups religious observance was generally based on tradition and cultural norms rather than on the formal initiation of individuals into the *Khalsa (amritdhari)* tradition. Thus, in their particular cases, lapses in the observance of the strict code of Sikh practices were not completely new or significant.

- Many Sikh immigrants were young males with a liberal educational background. The young are generally more critical of their traditional social and religious value systems, and opposed to concepts of traditional symbolic identity. Young Sikhs arriving in Britain were no exception. In the absence of family pressure to conform, they found it easy to break away from strict religious practices.

Despite the change in the collective as well as the individually visible Sikh identity, most of them retained their belief in Sikhism. Racial discrimination and free expression of anti-immigrant feelings in Britain raised their religious consciousness to levels even higher than it might have been in the Punjab.

Many Sikhs genuinely believed that becoming clean-shaven was only a temporary phase in their lives. They expressed the hope that, with a change in their situation in ın their return 'home' (which they all believed would happen one day), ḍ become observing Sikhs again. Their belief appears to have been partially realised. The majority of earlier Sikh immigrants are now either retired from employment or have been long-term unemployed. An increasing number of them have grown beards and started to wear turbans.

The re-unification of families and the inflow of male fiancées from the Punjab in the 1970s kept on enhancing the collective Sikh identity in Britain. The new male arrivals tended to preserve their turbans, showed more commitment to Sikh culture and traditions, and attended gurdwaras more frequently. Similarly, the arrival of Sikh migrants from East African countries in the late 1960s and early 70s, who tended to be more observant of the articles of the faith, made a significant impact on those who came to Britain directly from the Punjab.

The last two decades have witnessed an apparent revival in the desire of many individual Sikhs to return to the wearing of turbans and keeping uncut hair. In Bradford, for instance, many clean-shaven Sikhs who worked on public transport re-adopted turbans soon after the appointment of the first turbaned bus conductor in November 1968. Some important factors have contributed towards this reversal ın the earlier trend, and have encouraged adherence to traditional norms of appearance.

The commonly held belief of many Sikh migrants, that not wearing turbans would make them more accepted within the white host community, has proved false. On the other hand, by wearing turbans they feel at ease and enjoy more respect within their own community. A clear indication of this is an ever-increasing number of clean-shaven Sikhs wearing turbans during their visits to gurdwaras and on social occasions, such as weddings.

Many Sikh parents are concerned about the erosion of their children's commitment to religious values and visible Sikh identity, and a declining belief in their traditional social and religious values. Particularly, clean- shaven fathers see themselves as poor models for their own children. Such consciousness amongst parents has revived their own interest in traditional religious practices.

The increased visits of many *sant* (Sikh saints) and *parcharik* (preachers) and musicians from the Punjab have had a significant impact on their audiences in gurdwaras. They forcefully remind the congregations of the great traditions and values of the Sikh way of life. They have held *Amrit Parchar* sessions in which willing Sikhs are baptised en masse. A number of such sessions have been held in Bradford gurdwaras and some local Sikhs have attended such ceremonies to receive *Amrit* in other cities.

Major developments in the Punjab always affect the life and identity of Sikhs in the Diaspora in the last few decades. The Akali governments in the Punjab gave a very high profile to the celebrations of the 500th birth anniversary of Guru Nanak, the 300th anniversary of the martyrdom of Guru Teg Bahadur, the 300th birth anniversary of Guru Gobind Singh, and the 400th anniversary of the foundation of Amritsar, the Vatican City of the Sikhs. In most British cities, Sikhs celebrated these major events with great pomp and show. Such celebrations have dramaticaly raised the public profile of the local Sikh communities.

The most significant event, with serious and lasting influences on Sikh communities abroad, has been the 'Blue Star Operation', the Indian army attack on the Golden Temple in Amritsar, in June 1984. This focused the attention of the world's media on Sikh affairs in the Punjab and on the activities of Sikh communities overseas, particularly in Britain, Canada and the United States of America, for a considerable period of time. As a result of media coverage, Sikh identity has been sharply differentiated from Hindu identity.

In countries like Britain the concept of being an 'Indian' has become irrelevant and different sections of the Indian population display and stress the regional, religious and linguistic aspects of their ethnicity. For a number of years, strong anti-Indian government feelings among Sikhs prevailed. Anti-Hinduism sentiments were also expressed quite frequently and openly by many Sikh organisations.

Like other Sikhs in Britain, the Bradford Sikh population strongly condemned the actions and approach of the Indian Government in handling the events of 1984 in the Punjab. The strength of feelings however varied considerably within various groups in Britain as well as in Bradford. *Jat*-Sikhs were more militant and aggressive and were seen to be leading events. *Ramgarhias* showed intense feeling of hurt but remained cautious in openly expressing anti-Hindu or anti-Indian government views. *Ad-dharmis* or *Ravidasias* played a passive role and co-operated reluctantly in protests.

The intensification and radicalisation of Sikh identity during this period has had a number of significant results with some positive outcomes to what would otherwise be worrying and negative developments.

- Young people's interest in Sikh identity were significantly enhanced. More were attracted to gurdwara affairs and involved in the leadership than would have done otherwise.
- The local non-Sikh communities became more aware of the Sikh presence in Britain.
- These events generated a good deal of political activity within and without the Sikh community thus raising Sikhs' interest and confidence in the political processes in general.
- The serious turmoil in the Punjab provided a fresh opportunity for Sikh organisations and their leadership to remind ordinary Sikhs of past and current injustices and discrimination from which they suffer as a result of being a religious minority.

- Prior to 1984 leaders of most Sikh organisations were predominantly clean-shaven, *Sehajdharis*. Events during the 1980s raised a serious question about their right to hold positions in the management of gurdwaras and other religious organisations. It was argued that only persons who maintain the Sikh code of conduct and discipline should have the right to occupy positions of leadership. As a consequence, the leadership of some gurdwaras passed into the hands of young people, belonging to the militant and pro-Khalistan movements. In others, serious tensions arose and the *sangats* became fragmented.

Given the situation that a majority of ordinary Sikhs still have only a superficial knowledge of the basic principles and practices of their religion, and a merely popular view of Sikh history, the role of gurdwaras in the preservation and promotion of Sikh identity has been highlighted.

Religion and Sikh Youth

On days of religious celebrations, gatherings in gurdwaras are predominantly women, very young children and older men. Young people are generally conspicuous by their absence. The religious services in gurdwaras are conducted in Punjabi and most young children find these incomprehensible and of little interest to them. To the author's knowledge, at present, no gurdwara in Britain makes separate arrangements for religious instruction in English for young Sikhs. However, the Sikh Missionary Society (UK) hold an annual *gurmat camp* in the summer for youngsters to learn about *Gurbani* and Sikh religious practices.

Most young Sikhs apparently lack a formal religious upbringing and have undergone little instruction in Sikhism, unlike most Muslim children who attend mosques or madrasas for Islamic education. The limited knowledge Sikh children acquire about their religious beliefs and socio-cultural practices is mainly through participation in religious and social events in the family and the community.

In response to a question: "How important is religion to the way you live your life?" the latest PSI study by Modood et al, (1997, p. 301) discovered a marked generational difference among those who ticked the box "very important". The figure declined from two thirds among the oldest Sikhs to a third among the youngest Sikhs. Although nearly a half of all 16-34 year old Sikhs also answered "fairly important". Fourteen per cent of all Sikhs answered "not important" compared with only 4 % of Muslims and 11 % of Hindus. The authors also discovered that the proportion that answered "very important" declined among those with high qualifications, especially among Hindus and Sikhs.

The PSI study's findings also showed that only one in three of the Indians born in Britain (mainly Hindus and Sikhs) compared with more than half of the Muslims (Pakistani and Bangladeshi) thought that religion was important in their life. However, surprisingly, more than 70 % of Sikhs visit a gurdwara more than once a month. The difference in a high proportion of Sikhs visiting a gurdwara and a low proportion giving importance to the religion in their life is easily explained by the fact that many of them go to a gurdwara to attend social functions rather than for worship.

A reasonable conclusion appears to be that any revival of Sikh identity that has happened so far is mainly limited to the adult Sikh population in Britain. In the aftermath of the events of the 1980s, it was noticed that the number of Sikh boys in local schools wearing turbans and growing long uncut hair had increased. It was a passing phase created by external factors. With the easing of such pressures the younger generation of British Sikhs seems to be lapsing into a more lax attitude. All the indications so far suggest that they will retain the Sikh religion but with far less emphasis on *Khalsa* tradition and social customs and with diminished understanding and appreciation of Sikh beliefs.

Sikh parents and community leaders often articulate their concerns about the erosion of traditional values in the life styles and attitudes of young British Sikhs. Despite this awareness and concern, little effort is made to create facilities to meet the particular needs of young people or to involve them in community affairs. Therefore, the growing alienation of most British-born Sikhs from their religious tradition is understandable.

CHAPTER 8

WOMEN, MARRIAGES AND THE YOUNGER GENERATION

Sikh Women

Emigration to Britain changed the role, position and life styles of most Sikh women. With the exception of some professionally qualified women, the majority had little formal education before arriving in Britain. Most of them came as dependent wives, daughters, mothers and fiancées. Gradually, however, after their arrival in Britain many of them became workers. The majority found unskilled jobs in textiles and, with the emergence of Asian garment manufacturers in the 1970s, some became home-workers. As they grew in confidence and developed their communication skills in English, some got jobs in local mail order firms and other service industries. It is only in the last decade or so that a small minority, with educational and professional qualifications from the sub-continent, having acquired a reasonable command of English, have found jobs as nursery assistants in schools, and as interpreters and translators in clinics, hospitals and welfare offices. A substantial number are now self-employed in small family businesses.

Those who arrived during their school-going age and who, therefore, had some benefit from the British education system have managed to secure jobs as teachers of English as a second language, community language teachers or other jobs directly relating to multi-cultural education or as equal opportunities advisers in various organisations. More recently, a considerable number of young Sikh women, born and brought up in Britain, have gone into mainstream occupations such as medicine, accountancy, law and pharmacy. Whatever their status and position in the labour market, their contribution to the family income is considerable. Working women have helped most Sikh households to achieve a good standard of living. For themselves, they have earned dignity and status.

Work has given most Sikh women greater economic freedom in Britain. Their economic independence has resulted in them having a greater say in family financial decisions. The money in their pockets is the single most remarkable component of the post-migration experience of Sikh women in Britain. Whether the money comes from their husbands' pay packets or their own earnings or from social security benefits it has affected their position in the family. Many own property and investments in their own names. They can spend more money on themselves and provide an elaborate, varied and expensive dowry for themselves or for their daughters. This newly-achieved economic independence also means that they can sponsor their own parents, brothers or other members of their family for permanent settlement in Britain or for social visits which they could not have done previously without the consent of their husbands.

Work outside the home and access to the car for independent movement have tremendously affected the freedom of Sikh women to develop their own social contacts and do shopping on their own. Employment widens their horizon generally and enables them to develop confidence for independent survival. The problems of isolation and depression, so common among South Asian women confined to home, are far less among working Sikh women. (Boneham, 1989)

The age of marriage has been pushed higher both for girls and boys within Sikh families. The availability of the pill has liberated the younger generation of women to marry late and to pursue their educational and professional careers under less pressure from their parents. The likelihood of scandals and gossip within the community from the birth of children from pre-marriage liaisons is lessened. Women can plan to start a family with reduced pressures from the in-law's family and other relatives.

Sikh women in Britain have become more sophisticated and elegant in the choice of clothes they wear. They may wear a trouser suit at work, traditional *shalwar, kameez and dupata* at home, and colourful embroidered saris on social occasions like weddings. They seem to enjoy flaunting their newly acquired wealth by wearing heavy gold jewellery.

Sikh women play an important active part in the various community organisations, particularly in gurdwaras. Some Sikh women are also active in Asian women's organisations in the city. However, there is no exclusive Sikh women's organisation or community centre in Bradford. They are conspicuous by their presence in most public celebrations and protest marches. But not many are seen in leadership roles. Very few gurdwaras in Britain have even token women members in their management committees, none of the gurdwaras in Bradford have any. Reasons for their absence from the leadership of community organisations are complex. To a very large extent it is due to the patriarchal structure of Sikh society. In spite of the liberal cultural and religious traditions among Sikhs, and their western lifestyles, the majority of men still hold fairly conservative attitudes.

There is a lack of consistency and pattern in the position Sikh men accord to women or their female partners. To be more educated and modernised at a mental level does not necessarily imply or reflect a change in the traditional social norms about gender divisions. In fact, for social status and respectability, a man may revert to socially backward behaviour and award females a lower position; a position of carrying out traditional roles within the family and the larger community. For

Vaisakhi procession

example, many male Sikhs may intellectually accept, even welcome, a wife's higher education, a professional job or total emancipation, yet emotionally when the crunch comes they may unexpectedly manifest male chauvinism from the deep roots of male pride. The first generation of Sikh women, born and brought up within the traditional culture, can cope with this paradoxical behaviour more realistically in order to maintain harmony in married family life than can girls educated in Britain. For the latter, this often results in domestic and marital problems.

Joint mehfals of Sikh men and women are uncommon if not rare. Even among close friends preference is still for men and women to gossip in separate groups. Female mehfals are more confined to gossip about youngsters' marriages, marriage failures, extra marital sexual relations and the breakdown in relationships within family situations. Talk about clothes, the latest fashions in garments and jewelry and a critical assessment of gurdwara activities dominate the conversation in their gatherings. High politics is left alone in their mehfals. Women share misfortunes within families in the circle of their contact more sympathetically. However, small groups can be 'very bitchy' about other women. Interestingly, it is becoming common among Sikh men and women, young and old, to dance together when bhangra music is played at wedding celebrations or at other social events.

Elderly Sikh women play an important role in the preservation and propagation of traditional social customs. Most of them display a strong commitment to religious and cultural practices and social norms compared with that displayed by men and younger women. In all South Asian communities in Britain, women are perceived as the 'izzat' (honour) of a family and 'pride' of a community. Any wrong move on their part is seen as tarnishing the family name and letting the whole community down. Thus, attitudes and modes of behaviour which are becoming more and more liberal and independent usually cause tensions within a family and the community. This puts an enormous pressure on Sikh girls and their parents to conduct their lives within standards of behaviour traditionally acceptable to the community.

Marriages

A significant change has come about in the arrangement of marriages and the observance of traditional marriage practices and celebrations. Now, in Sikh families, very few traditionally arranged marriages take place. Over the years young Sikh girls have achieved a much greater say in the choice of their marriage partners. Sikhs have almost abandoned the practice of finding marriage partners for their children from Punjab. It is largely due to three factors.

- Firstly, the sponsoring of economic migration in the guise of getting male fiancés from the close network of relatives in the Punjab has become difficult due to the tightening up of immigration rules for this category.
- Secondly, experience has shown that the marriages arranged in this way are proving unstable, and are resented and resisted by children born and grown up Britain.
- Thirdly, unlike Muslims, Sikhs do not have the obligation or cultural tradition of marrying close cousins.

The most worrying trend is a gradual increase in unsuccessful marriages. Incidences of marriage breakdowns and divorces are on the increase. It is not implied that unsuccessful marriages are a direct consequence of the changes in the pattern of traditional system of arranged marriages. In the past, there was great pressure placed upon a woman to preserve her marriage at any cost. Perhaps, with some economic independence, they are no longer prepared to put up with unfair treatment on their husbands' part or by their in-laws. Even when most marriages are agreed through the mutual consent of partners and parents on both sides, their success rate is on the decline. Family or community pressure to keep unhappy marriages going no longer works.

The tradition of blessing the newly married couple with presents of clothes, jewellry and kitchenware has almost entirely been replaced by cash gifts from their relatives. A dowry, if any, has become a private affair between two families. Wedding receptions have become more elaborate, larger and, hence, more expensive. Live group music, a popular form of entertainment at most weddings in the 1980s and early 1990s, is gradually loosing its popularity and DJs are becoming more common. Surprisingly, many old customs, rites and rituals, and ceremonies relating to wedding celebrations, almost ignored in contemporary Punjab, are performed in Britain more routinely and strictly. Hence, wedding celebrations are spread over a number of days. Honeymoons, stag nights and hen parties are taking hold fast. Punjabi marriages have become a strange blend of tradition and modernity. An interesting fusion of eastern and western wedding practices.

Parental Perception of the Younger Generation

The subject of British-born children occupies a major proportion of time in most Sikh mehfals. Among the major concerns of parents are the changing attitudes of their British-born children. Such changes are discussed in a love-hate manner. Negative and positive aspects are always mingled. Their achievements in education and employment are bragged about. The development of 'individualism', for example, is deplored. The inevitability of some change seems to be expected and is painfully accepted. With the fear of losing face and honour of the family, problems and negative attitudes of one's children are difficult to disclose outside the immediate family. Therefore, mehfals offer opportunities to express individual feelings of hurt, disappointment and frustration without personalising the issues.

Children with non-English speaking parents have considerable power over their parents. In many families they have complete access to knowledge about family finances, saving accounts, health problems and so on as they act as interpreters or even as decision-makers. In many situations, when parents feel that their youngsters are taking undue advantage of their limitations in dealing with officials or local institutions or of their dependence on their children in normal life activities, they often over-react or become bossy. Such bossiness is actually a manifestation of parent's helplessness and feelings of inferiority. The normal consequence of this behaviour is yet more conflict with their children.

Most parents see their children as compulsive spenders, outgoing, leisure loving, with many of them unconcerned about their future life, showing no particular interest in saving for the future or for the traditional social commitments within a family. They are criticised for being self-centred, selfish and for their narrow view of family. Youngsters' general lack of concern about what their relatives and members of the community may think about their behaviour is not appreciated. Their individualistic thinking and independent decision-making approach to life contrasts sharply with their parents' experience.

Children hold a very different view about values such as izzat, respect and status to those of their parents. They display more confidence and optimism about their survival and success in Britain. To the disappointment of parents they show little interest in the wealth and properties of their families in Punjab to which they are entitled. Parents feel upset to hear children's critical comments on their conservative and reactionary attitudes. Parents' nostalgic view of a Punjab they left behind and their attachment to the ancestral home makes little sense to the children. The only comforting thing to the parents is their children's willingness to visit home and relatives in the Punjab for short stays as on holiday destinations.

Many Sikh parents do not have access to their young people's collective thoughts. During the last few decades a very strong technologically-buttressed western culture, with all the might of the mass media, multiplicity of TV channels, videos, Internet etc., has impacted on the thinking and behaviour of the British born Sikh generation leaving their parents in a totally baffled state. In Britain, young Sikhs negotiate their own identities in mixed peer groups. Furthermore, they internalise styles, speech and communication patterns that are dominant in the localities in which they are situated. They imbibe in their identities regional, class and ethnic codes in some modified way. Therefore, they are in a continuous process of constructing and reconstructing their identities. (Bhachu, 1991) As many of the young Sikhs still live within close proximity of their concentrated communities the western orientation of their social activities has become a concern and a source of shame for many parents.

Overall, the younger generation of Sikhs is working hard to obtain an acceptable balance between individual freedom and the achievement of personal aspirations on the one hand, and the collectivity of the family, in which individual achievements (or any failures) are seen as the achievements of the whole family, on the other. The *izzat* of the family is still of primary importance to the parents, with individual dignity and status subservient to the enhancement of this. Thus, happiness and misery for most Sikh parents are determined by how their own community judge their children's position in life.

CHAPTER 9

EDUCATION, LANGUAGE AND CULTURE

Education

Sikh migrants have demonstrated a high degree of commitment to obtaining education for self-advancement in Britain. On the whole, their attitude towards education is very pragmatic. They seek qualifications and work-oriented education for reasons of social mobility, both in terms of class and caste. Their minority status reinforces their desire to pursue vocational education in order to ensure their future success in Britain. These high educational aspirations are not restricted to a particular class group or a caste group. (Bhachu, 1985a and Singh, 1985)

In the 1970s a number of educated Sikhs in the city sent their sons for public school education in India. This trend was particularly noticed among those working on the city buses. This was a repetition of the story of previous Sikh migrant communities in East African countries and Fiji, who usually sent their children to India for higher education. It basically demonstrated their desire and belief that they would return "home" one day and that was where their children's future lay. Their newly acquired financial capability, they believed, would enable their children to receive the best education in India, which in turn would provide them with the opportunity to obtain higher level prestigious jobs in India. As the results of this approach proved unsatisfactory, the trend reversed very quickly with children being sent, in increasing numbers, to fee-paying local private schools.

Among Sikhs, the education of girls at all levels is considered equally as important as for boys. For example, in 1982, 5 % of all Sikh women in Britain were in full-time education compared to 4 % of Muslim women and 6 % of Hindu women. (Brown, 1984). Education is considered important for girls as a preparation for careers as well as to improve their chances in the 'marriage market'. Unlike Muslim parents in Britain, Sikhs have no serious religious objections to girls attending mixed schools.

However, they may prefer single-sex schools purely to protect their girls from developing friendships or sexual relations with boys, particularly with boys of different castes or religions. They have given very little public support to Muslim organisations demanding single-sex schools in Bradford.

The attitude and approach of Sikh parents towards such general schooling issues as school uniforms, school meals, mixed classes for physical education and games, and religious education, have been fairly practical and accommodating. Very rarely have they confronted the normal rules. However, Sikh children have faced difficulties in securing the right to wear some of the visible symbols of the Sikh faith and identity in schools e.g. turbans, steel bracelets and ceremonial swords. Despite the fact that Sikhs have won the legal right to wear a turban in schools, parents usually allow their boys to take them off, if they choose to do so, when taking part in games, swimming and P.E. lessons.

For Sikh boys western dress presents no problem but opinion on the matter of dress for girls varies. Sikh parents do not object to western dress for girls on religious grounds, but for them it is a departure from the traditional dress for Punjabi women, i. e. a *dupata, shalwar* and a *kameez*. Despite their strong reluctance initially, the wearing of skirts by Sikh girls in schools raises no serious concern from their parents. However, most Sikh parents still disapprove of girls taking part in sports activities, in mixed teams, and wearing the usual attire of shorts and blouses. Unlike some members of the Muslim Parents Association in Bradford, who threatened to withdraw their daughters from schools on the matter of school dress for girls, Sikh parents have never expressed their concern so strongly. They appear to have accepted the situation, not through choice, but as a part of the general process of westernisation in their overall life styles.

The Sikhs have no serious restrictions in the choice of food, except that they are forbidden to eat meat prepared by ritual slaughter (*halal*). However, Sikhs, like Hindus, are religiously forbidden to eat beef. In schools, if Sikh children have problems with food, it is not because of their religion, but due to a personal dislike of western food or the way it is cooked. On the other hand, many Sikh children are becoming fussy about food cooked in the Asian way at home and prefer less spicy food. In reality Sikh parents have been pragmatic in letting their children eat the food they like in schools but do prefer them not to eat beef. (Drury, 1991) Unlike Muslim parents they have never made school food a high profile public issue.

In the early 1980s, Bradford Local Education Authority developed a very positive policy towards the introduction of multi-cultural education in schools and for dealing with the particular needs of South Asian children. General guidelines issued on various aspects of its multicultural policy in education, reasonably followed by schools, have lessened some of the South Asian parents' concerns.

In the socio-religious aspect of school life Sikh children have posed very few problems. Sikh parents have never made school religious assemblies a matter of serious concern. On the whole, they have argued in favour of multi-faith religious education in schools, for the benefit of all children, including their own. They appreciate the currently offered arrangement for instruction in Sikhism for Sikh children under the LEA's policy.

The experience in Bradford suggests that it is the Muslim parents and their organisations that have been leading the debate on issues concerning the education of their children in schools and Sikhs and Hindus seem to have passively followed them. For instance, in the 1970s, the Muslim Parents' Association in Bradford objected to the informal school environment being "immoral and anti-Muslim". It described the schooling system as "indoctrination of Muslim children to the values of Western society and erosion of traditional Muslim values about role of women, respect for family and parents". They were objecting to the participation of girls in school activities e.g., drama, and dance, fund-raising functions, sex education lessons, swimming, mixed games and physical education classes.

In the early 1980s, the Bradford Council of Mosques vigorously campaigned for the provision of 'halal meat' in schools, the teaching of Urdu in mainstream schools, financial assistance to supplementary schools run by the Muslim community, and the teaching of Islam in schools to Muslim children by Muslim teachers. On these issues, Sikh and Hindu organisations supported the Muslim organisation but have not fought for such provision with the same ferocity on their own. Pakistani Muslims, being the majority ethnic group locally, have their own elected members on the City Council, hold strong religious convictions, and have gained considerable success in these areas. All ethnic minority groups, including the Sikhs, have benefited from the multi-cultural education policies of the LEA.

The establishment of separate religious schools for Sikh children has never been a priority for Sikhs in Britain. In 1971, a meeting in Gravesend (Kent) discussed the question of establishing a Khalsa school for Sikh children. It was argued that such a school would enable their children to fully develop their educational and vocational capabilities which discrimination in mainstream schools denied them. It would also help to inculcate and maintain young peoples' interest in their religion, culture and social values. Furthermore, it would safeguard their girls, the bearers of family 'izzat' (honour) from pollution. The case for a separate school was lost on the major argument that such a provision would deny Sikh children a comprehensive knowl- edge of the English language, culture, social values and norms, and thus hindering their progress in maximising their opportunities for success in life. It was emphasised that the duty of meeting the religious and cultural needs of young people and par- ticularly that of safeguarding girls rested primarily with the family and gurdwaras, and not with schools. (Helwig, 1979, p. 109)

Since then, two unsuccessful attempts (in 1978 and 1980) have been made by Sikhs from Southall to create a Khalsa School. (Taylor and Hegarty, 1985, p. 378) Today, there are two voluntary Khalsa Schools in the country, one in Hays and the second one in Chigwell, started in the early 1990s. In Bradford, Sikhs have never raised the question of a Khalsa school.

On the important issue of separate, religious grant-aided voluntary schools, Sikhs and Muslims appear to have somewhat different approaches. In 1983, the Bradford Muslim Parents' Association applied to the Department of Education and Science, to turn five schools with predominantly Muslim intake into grant-aided schools for Muslims. Their application was rejected and it did not have the support of the more representative and influential Muslim organisation, the Bradford Council of Mosques. At present there is one private school for Muslim girls (that is seeking voluntary-aided status) in the city and there are many more in the country. In the absence of a public debate on the issue, it is difficult to speculate on the reasons for Sikhs' lack of enthusiasm for separate religious schools. Sikhs have continuously expressed concerns on issues such as

· Discrimination in schools and the labour market.
· The marginalisation of Sikh religion, history, social and religious values in the multi-faith approach to religious education and general curriculum in schools.
· Girls developing more western, independent and secular attitudes.

The main arguments against establishing separate religious schools would be the divisive nature of such schools and the risks involved in achieving the high quality of education needed for economic success and social mobility in mainstream British society to which the Sikhs aspire.

In the Fourth National Survey of Ethnic Minorities in 1994 (Modood et al, 1997, pp. 324-325) only 9 % of all Sikhs indicated a preference for schools of one's own religion against 6 % of Hindus and 25 % of Muslims respondents. Again only 20 % of Sikhs supported religious schools in the state sector. (Sixty one per cent of Sikhs do not support religious schools within the state sector against a much lower figure of 28 % of Muslim, and a higher figure of 72 % of Hindu respondents).

The educational achievements of Sikh children in Bradford seem to be quite impressive when compared with the performance of children of other South Asian communities. For example, an analysis of examination results of ethnic minority pupils in Braford for the period 1995-97, concludes that pupils of Indian origin (which includes Sikhs) were entered for more subjects than any other group in the GCSE examinations and a higher percentage of them (almost 40 %) consistently achieved five-plus A-C Grade passes in the examination even compared with white pupils (almost 28 %). Similarly, a significantly higher proportion of Indian pupils stayed at school to take A level courses and they were the highest scoring ethnic group in those examinations. The average score of Indian girls was even higher than the boys' score.[1] In my view, part of the explanation for a relatively higher success rate for young Sikhs in education and careers may lie in their parents' overall pragmatic approach to education.

Language

Alongside English, Panjabi is the language of day to day communication for over two thirds of the South Asians in Britain. It is a shared language between Sikhs, Punjabi Hindus and the majority of Pakistani Muslims. Panjabi holds a special significance for the Sikhs, as their religious scriptures are in this language. Panjabi-speaking Muslims and Hindus do not normally use Panjabi for written communication, particularly Panjabi written in the Gurmukhi script. For written communication Hindus prefer Hindi, which is associated with Hinduism and is also the national language of India. Likewise, Urdu is associated with Islam and is the national language of Pakistan. Those Pakistanis, who write in Panjabi, use the Persian script. Sikhs educated in the Punjab are more likely to be able to read and write Hindi and many first generation Sikhs may even be able to read and write Urdu.

Panjabi is still the dominant spoken language within most Sikh family and community settings. However, the children limit their use of Panjabi to conversations with their parents and other adults in situations where discourse in English would not be not possible. Children rarely converse in Panjabi among themselves. When they do use it, interestingly, they construct their sentences with English words and phrases neatly slotted into the appropriate places. There is also a tendency among youngsters to use certain Panjabi words in an anglicised manner in their mutual conversation in English. Their comprehension of Panjabi is generally much better than their own spoken usage of the language.[2]

Sikh parents demonstrate a profound desire to teach Panjabi to their children. They understand its vital role in the preservation of their traditional culture, the maintenance of strong relations within the family and links with relatives in India, and above all their religious heritage. However, it appears that Panjabi, as a language of common discourse, is not likely to last beyond the life of the present adult generation. The reading of Panjabi books and newspapers is uncommon among children. Even those who may have studied Panjabi at school or in gurdwara classes, or have taken GCSE or 'A' Level examinations in it, do not generally read any material available in Panjabi.

The issues relating to the retention of the Panjabi language and religious education are equally vital to the Sikh community. At present, arrangements for the teaching of Panjabi exist in almost all gurdwaras in Britain. Generally the classes are held at the weekends. Panjabi has also been introduced as a second language for all children or as a community language for Panjabi-speaking children in some of the state schools in cities where a concentration of Sikhs exists. For example, in Bradford in 1997 ten students from state schools achieved A-C GCSE grade passes. A further 75 students took the GCSE examination through gurdwara supplementary schools with a success rate of 90 per cent. These arrangements have affected the Sikh identity very positively.

Panjabi Journalism

Panjabi journalism in Britain is well established. From a large number of Panjabi weeklies and monthlies started since the mid 1960s the current survivors are, Des Pardes, the Punjab Times and Awaze Quam. All these weeklies are widely read by Sikhs in Bradford. In the absence of a local Panjabi newsletter, gurdwaras and other Sikh organisations use these papers for advertising their events and activities. These advertisements are more often an 'image boosting' measure, used by organisations and their leaders. The close knit nature of the local Sikh community where news spreads fairly fast through word of mouth, does not justify the expense of using national weeklies to disseminate information of purely local interest.

No regular Panjabi newspaper or community newsletter is published in Bradford. Two known attempts have been made in the past. Kiran, a weekly paper was started in 1967 by Raghbir Virdee, a local teacher, but ceased publication after a few issues. Similarly, the proprietor of Zamindar Travel, Malkiat Singh Takhar, started a monthly, Nari Sansar, which did not survive more than a few years. There are no well-known established Panjabi writers currently living in Bradford. However, Raghbir Dhand, a renowned Panjabi short story writer lived in Bradford for over twenty years before moving to Leeds prior to his death in December, 1990. Mohan Singh Kukarpindia, author of about ten novels has lived in the city since the early1960s. There is no known local Panjabi literary society in existence either. However, the Bradford Educational and Cultural Association of Sikhs (previously the Bradford Sikh Parents Association) have been organising regular Panjabi poetry readings since 1984.

Gathering at a Kavi Darbar (poetry reading) in Bradford

A number of developments in the life of British Sikhs has prolonged the maintenance of Panjabi in Britain. An increase in the celebration of social and religious events with enhanced emphasis on traditional rites, rituals and customs is encouraging the use of the Panjabi language and, therefore, a desire to learn it. An enhanced interest within the community in Panjabi folk songs, music, bhangra dance, local melas, Panjabi film videos, annual sports tournaments is offering new opportunities, particularly for the youngsters, to use their Panjabi. Events in the Punjab in the 1980s and the celebrations of the Tri-Centenary of the Birth of Khalsa (1999) have made a very positive impact on Punjabi identity in Britain, and created a new interest in the Panjabi language. Local libraries keep a good stock of Panjabi books on a wide variety of subjects. Most gurdwaras also hold a limited number of Panjabi books, on a narrow range of topics, for their readers. However, the library stocks remain underused and enthusiasm for borrowing books, particularly among young people, is low. All the indications are that Panjabi will survive as a community language well into the first quarter of the next century. Punjabi culture, however, may survive even longer, but in a much-modified form. The Panjabi language may retain its role only in the performance of religious rites on certain social occasions.

Culture

Sikhs have contributed to the religious and cultural mosaic of Britain in a number of ways. The visible identity of the local Sikh populations adds to the religious diversity of major cities where they have settled. For example, six Sikh temples, four of those in highly visible prominent locations close to Bradford city centre, not only serve as places of worship for the Sikh community but can be of great interest to foreign visitors to the city, particularly from countries which have no Sikh communities of their own. Since 1987, in April each year, Bradford Sikhs celebrate their Vaisakhi function with great pomp and show. Hundreds of local Sikhs parade (called Nagar Kirtan) on the roads of the inner city. These parades present a great colourful spectacle and are a source of entertainment for all Bradfordians. Diwali celebrations with their big fireworks displays also add to the festivities for all.

With the consolidation of the community in the 1960s, Asian business entrepreneurs established cinemas showing Indian films at the weekends. As the community became more prosperous, the same businessmen started inviting famous singers and other artists from the sub-continent to entertain their more affluent clients. Music concerts presented by visiting artists from other parts of the UK or the Indian sub-continent are still very popular and have become more frequent. Such concerts, although primarily organised for the local South Asian communities, also attract audiences from the wider local population as a whole.

In the 1980s the Sikh community in Britain witnessed the emergence of a variety of musical entertainment groups. Performances by bhangra dance groups and groups of young Punjabi singers became an integral part of all cultural functions and social occasions. Although the trend has somewhat slowed down, a number of such groups are now well established in Britain. Punjabi folk music and bhangra are extremely popular with both young Sikh men and women. The Punjabi bhangra dance seems to have earned a permanent position in all local celebrations, for instance, whether it is the Queen's visit to the city, a charity show or the annual Bradford Festival (Mela).

The first known musical group in Bradford, Ujjala, was established under the guidance of Mohinder Singh Khinda, a professional musician and singer in the late 1970s. The group still exists and performs at small social functions. Now some more groups have emerged in Bradford.

Nachda Punjab Bhangra group performing for HRH the Queen 1997

The Anjana group has been around for almost two decades. The group members come from a variety of musical backgrounds, e g Indian folk and classical music, English and Irish traditional music. Their performances reflect an unusual mixture of styles with a miscellany of musical instruments. The group has given performances throughout Britain at Punjabi weddings, arts festivals, in the Bradford

Mela, and even the occasional public house. The group has recorded a number of albums.

Four young and enthusiastic musicians from Bradford and Leeds formed Sansar, a bhangra band, in the early days of 1994. The group has given numerous shows up and down the country in its fairly short life. In addition to its routine performances at weddings, melas and other Asian festivals, the group participated in BBC2's Young Musicians programme and Breakfast TV News Extra in June 1996. The group is a regular contributor to the Bradford Annual Festival (Mela). It has also released an album of its Panjabi songs.

Nachda Punjab is Bradford's best known bhangra group and has given performances on TV. The group has taken part in a number of national performances and festivals and won awards. It staged a show in honour of Her Majesty the Queen during her visit to Bradford in 1997.

Sports Tournaments

Every summer there are sports tournaments in major cities of Sikh concentration in Britain. These events are advertised in the Panjabi weeklies and attract big crowds. Kabadi, a Punjabi game, is a special feature of these tournaments. There is now a national British Kabbadi Federation which oversees and co-ordinates these tournaments in most of the cities. It also sends British Kabadi teams abroad and make reciprocal arrangements for the teams from other countries to visit Britain. Teams from all over England participate in these events.

In Bradford, The Guru Nanak Charitable Trust was set up in 1981 by Mewa Singh Bassan, a local JP, with the help of a multi-racial board of trustees. The Trust bought an unused clinic in Usher Street and established an indoor sports centre there. On two occasions it organised muti-racial sports events for school children in the early eighties. Later, the centre was converted into a restaurant and since then not much has been heard of Trust's sporting activities.

Indian United Sports Club (Bradford) was set up in the early 1970s to promote sporting activities within the community. It organised annually, a sports tournament in the city for a few years with the help of local gurdwaras and donations from the public. The annual event continues but not under the auspices of the same club. For a number of years the Ramgharia Sikh Temple had its own hockey and volley ball teams. Guru Nanak Gurdwara has established a sports hall of its own where sporting activities are organised by an active management team of young Sikhs.

A kabadi match in Bradford

CHAPTER 10

LIVING IN A MULTI-RACIAL, MULTI-ETHNIC
AND MULTI-FAITH SOCIETY

Sikhs and the White Community

Bradford takes pride in receiving immigrants of various nationalities at different stages of its industrial development. It also claims to have been a peaceful home for them, most of the time. As a consequence of continuous changes in the local population, it is now a multi-cultural, multi-lingual and multi-faith city. The Irish, German Jews, people from Eastern European countries, African-Caribbeans and South Asians, all have contributed to the present cultural make-up of the city. Relations between such ethnically diverse groups are facilitated or inhibited by a complex set of factors such as,

- · the nature of historical links between the communities,
- · linguistic differences,
- · distinctive cultural and religious characteristics,
- · opportunities available for social interaction,
- · individual group motivations,
- · the length and permanency of contact, and
- · positive / negative assessments of each other's values and norms of life.

The nature and level of integration in 'the private domain' and 'the public domain' generally differ. For example, in private spheres such as choice of marriage partners, friends and leisure activities, individual considerations, within the boundaries of one's ethnic group, are usually more important.

Social interactions are always dynamic. This is particularly the case with South Asian immigrants in Britain. On arrival they had to conduct their lives in a new society with significantly different social, cultural and religious norms and values. They found the industrial work environment unfamiliar. For them, most British labour and political institutions were new. They faced a social and political environment of general resentment and hostility.

The relations between local whites and first generation Sikh migrants can be best described as of a 'market place' type. Their only interaction with local whites was as workers, consumers of products and recipients of services provided by private organisations and public sector agencies. Even at work, most of the time they worked in 'ethnic units', working with people of their own social and cultural backgrounds. Social interaction at work normally finished at the factory gates.

Only infrequently did contacts from the place of work turn into social friendships - usually sharing drinks in a pub at the weekends. White people's homes remained their own castles and out of bounds for their new workmates. Thus, most older generation Sikhs remained and are still insulated from significant contact with white communities. Their knowledge of the religious, social and cultural values of local white communities is simply the television version of British life styles.

Most first generation Sikhs are critical of the local practice of finding a marriage partner through trial and error. They condemn explicit sex, promiscuity, and gay and lesbian partnerships. They see the contemporary social issues concerning lone parents, single mothers, aids, drugs and the lack of parental control over children, as the product of western life styles. Such a negative evaluation of some trends in the British way of life influences the development of their personal friendships with members of white communities.

Right up to the end of the 1970s, Sikh children in the city had very limited opportunities to develop personal friendships with children of communities other than their own. Most of them attended schools away from their homes under the Local Education Authority's 'dispersal policy'. Thus, for them, the contact with white children was limited to school hours only. The rest of their life was spent in their own community neighbourhoods. The abolition of the dispersal policy in the early eighties and a fairly speedy movement of Sikhs out of the traditional areas of South Asian concentration in the city increased the opportunities for their children to develop stable friendships outside their own community groups. Furthermore, the widening of career choices by young Sikhs and their increased participation in higher education helped to enhance their opportunities for cross community dealings.

The younger generation's experience today is much different from that of their parents. They can operate across communities with growing confidence and effectiveness. The presence of white people at many Sikh weddings and social occasions, for example, is an obvious sign of increased cross community friendships.

The Sikhs as people are commonly regarded as liberal, informal and hospitable. Although individual attitudes and qualities are central when forming personal friendships, yet these general group characteristics facilitate the process of fostering social relations. Even after half a century of Sikh presence in the city, the inter- community mixing is not as high as it could have been expected. An overall conservative and cautious attitude of local whites in fostering friendships with outsiders may be partially responsible for it.

Most of the Sikh organisations in the city have made deliberate efforts, even if limited, to involve local white people in their religious and social activities. Local dignitaries such as leaders of the major political parties, Members of Parliament, key officials of the local authority and other public sector services, and leaders of other faiths have frequently been invited to major community functions. For example, Edward Lyons, M P for Bradford West, laid the foundation stone of Guru Gobind Singh Gurdwara. Parties of students from local schools and colleges, and groups from local churches and other organisations, are regularly received by all the local gurdwaras.

Strangely, however, little initiative has been shown by Sikh organisations to introduce their own community to the functioning of major local social and religious institutions. When invited, they have willingly and actively participated in most of the multi-faith services in the city. How much of this involvement has been voluntary and community inspired, and how much is political expediency, is difficult to assess. Undoubtedly, some political considerations influence the Sikh leaders' response to events external to their own community.

Overall, the current level of interaction may appear superficial and unbalanced, but it could provide a sound foundation on which to build better and deeper community relations in the future. It is also a clear indicator of Sikh aspirations for some social and civic integration.

Relations with Hindus

Despite some fundamental differences in religious beliefs and ways of worship, the Sikhs and Punjabi Hindus share a common language, culture, festivals and many social customs. The sense of Sikh separateness is strongest among the Amritdhari Sikhs who bear the five symbols of Sikhism and it is weak among Sehajdhari Sikhs, who do not display these symbols. Moreover, the religious boundaries between some lower caste groups from the Punjab, for example, chamars are less definite. Members of the same family in these groups may have Hindu as well as Sikh names.

In Bradford, Punjabi Hindus, fairly small in numbers, are widely diffused in settlement among the Sikhs. Most of the time the two communities celebrate some social and religious festivals together, as they usually did in India. Sikhs also contributed generously towards the building of the Hindu Temple on Leeds Road.

Social interaction between Sikhs and Gujarati Hindus, a larger group than the Punjabi Hindus in Britain, is very limited. Despite their common origin from India, their cultures, life styles, and community languages are different. They are also located physically separate from the areas of Sikh concentrations in most of the cities in Britain. In the 1960s and the early 70s, when the size of the Gujarati community in Bradford was relatively small, it frequently used gurdwara facilities for their social functions. On the whole, contact between the Sikh and Gujarati communities in the city has always been limited and superficial.

Hindus and Sikhs in the Punjab have always been divided on political issues such as the status of the Panjabi language, the creation of an autonomous state for Sikhs, and the presence of discrimination against Sikhs in general. As these sources of traditional conflict are less relevant in Britain, most of the time, there has been no serious religious antagonism between these groups. They have lived together in complete harmony. Nevertheless, the political events in the Punjab have always impacted on the strength of the relations between the two groups.

For example, the relations between the two communities in Britain became very tense and fragile during the eighties after the 1984 events in India. [1] Although, no serious incidents of hostility occurred in Bradford, yet very strong anti-Hindu and anti-Indian Government feelings were publicly expressed by the Sikhs in the city as elsewhere in the country. In August 1984, members of the Bradford branch of the International Sikh Youth Federation organised a big protest demonstration and picketed the weekend long International Conference of Hindus in the city, organised by the Vishwa Hindu Parishad. However, serious clashes were avoided. Despite the severe tensions between the two communities the formal relations between them did not completely break down.

Photograph by kind permission of the Telegraph & Argus, Bradford

An anti-Indian Government demonstration of Bradford Sikhs at the Vishwa Hindu Parishid conference in the city.

The personal relationships between individual Sikhs and Hindus remained cordial. Turmoil in Punjabi politics has continued in recent years but it appears that the social relations between the two communities, ruptured by the events of 1984, have been repaired to a large extent. However, the awareness of separate Sikh and Hindu identities has been firmly established and deepened among the members of both communities, and in the minds of the British public.

Relations with Muslims

Sikhs and the majority of Punjabi Muslims in Bradford come from a similar cultural background, speak the same language, share some dress and dietary patterns, and social notions of izzat (honour) and biradari (a close social network). It is the Islamic religious beliefs and some distinctive social and cultural features of the Muslim communities in Britain that separate them from the Sikh community.

The general attitude of the Sikhs towards Muslims is still very much coloured by the legacy of historical events. The horrific acts of persecution of Sikhs by Muslim rulers in the eighteenth century and the torturing to death of two of their two gurus are kept afresh in the minds of the Sikhs by the preachers in gurdwaras.[2] The partition of the Punjab in 1947, at the end of British rule in India, involved the transfer of populations between India and Pakistan, based on religion. It resulted in bloody religious riots in which thousands of people lost their lives and added a fresh dimension to the already historically antagonistic state of social relations between the Sikhs and Hindus on one side and the Muslims on the other. Since Partition, for most of the Sikhs and Pakistani Muslims, living side by side as close neighbours is a new experience.

In the earlier years of South Asian immigration into the city, the settlement pattern of the newcomers showed little evidence of a religious divide. However, over the years and with the reuniting of families, a significant separation has occurred in the physical location of these two communities. Sikhs have gradually moved out from their initial residential areas such as Thornbury, Laisterdyke, Bradford Moor and West Bowling, making room for Muslim families from the Manningham and Lumb Lane areas to move in. Now the spatial divide between the two communities is marked and evident. The present position is a consequence of a complex set of economic, social as well as religious factors. It has very little influence on the social relations between Sikhs and Muslims in Bradford, as social mixing between them was always limited.

At the community level relations between the two communities have normally remained harmonious. Even in potentially explosive situations mutual respect and peace was maintained between the two communities. For instance, when India and Pakistan were at war in 1965 and in 1971 when India sided with East Pakistan in seeking independence from West Pakistan to become Bangladesh, despite serious tension in the 'air', no incident of conflict occurred. However, such events have always pushed the two communities further apart.

It is difficult to speculate on the future attitudes and reactions of the different religious communities towards social mixing between their members. Inter-religious marriages are likely to remain unacceptable in the foreseeable future. However, social relations and free mixing of the younger members of all religious communities growing up together in the city are likely to increase. During the last few years, some serious clashes between Sikh and Muslim groups in places like Southall, Slough, Isleworth and Birmingham have been reported in the media. Most of these incidents involved young people from local colleges of further education. However, no such incident has so far happened in Bradford.

Contributions to Race and Community Relations

Bradford Sikhs have consistently and profoundly contributed towards fostering harmonious relations between various communities in the city. In addition to the cross-community activities of various Sikh organisations, their major contribution to local race relations has been through their active participation in the Bradford Racial Equality Council (REC), previously known as the Community Relations Council. The contribution has largely come through a small number of individuals, fully supported by the main Sikh organisations. For example, the author was centrally involved in the establishment of the Advisory Council for Commonwealth Citizens in 1966, the parent body of the present REC and has continued his involvement in the REC's activities over the last 33 years in various capacities. He chaired its Education Panel from 1972-84, the crucial period in the development of the multi-cultural policies of the Local Education Authority, before handing it over to Ranjit Kaur Arora. He also served the organisation as chairman in 1984-85. Two other Sikhs, Govinder Singh Dhaliwal (1991-1993) and Balbir Singh JP (1995-1998) had also been chairmen of the Bradford REC.

Leaders of the Sikh, Muslim and Hindu communities have always maintained good contacts which has proved very productive in times of tension. In 1986, the Federation of Bradford Sikh Organisations, the Bradford Council of Mosques and the Vishwa Hindu Parishad set up a Joint Committee of South Asian Organisations in Bradford. The Committee (now defunct) met fairly regularly for a number of years to discuss issues of common concern to the South Asian communities in the city. During the "Rushdie Affair" in the early 1990s, both Sikh and Hindu communities took a neutral political stance. By making no negative comment on the Muslim protest and the burning of Salman Rushdie's book, *The Satanic Verses*, they lent public support to the Muslim community which had become the focus of attack from many corners. Furthermore, the Indian Government's stand on the Kashmir issue and their handling of the Punjab crisis involving Sikhs in the Eighties have created some feelings of mutual sympathy and understanding between Sikhs and Muslims.

Since the demise of the Joint Council of South Asian Organisations, the leaders of all faith communities in the city have been meeting regularly as an informal forum under the chairmanship of the Bishop of Bradford, David Smith.

Despite facing serious prejudice and discrimination in employment, housing and in other spheres, Sikhs in Bradford have kept a low profile. Only on a very few occasions have they organised any major public demonstrations to express their particular concerns. Even during their protests against the 'bussing policy' of the Local Education Authority and the struggle for the right to wear turbans by transport employees and bakery workers, they followed a peaceful, rational path of negotiations.

Participation in Political and Civic Life

Right from their arrival in Britain Sikhs have been participating in political activities, initially largely through the Indian Workers Associations (IWAs). IWAs were close allies of major groups campaigning against racial discrimination, right-wing anti-immigration and anti-immigrants groups, and racially discriminatory policies and immigration legislation. The IWA's socialist political and economic idealogy attracted its leadership to the British Labour Party. Many of them joined the Party and encouraged their members to do the same. Most of the Sikhs became and still remain Labour Party voters in local and national elections. However, they themselves did not aspire to become candidates in these elections in any significant numbers until the late 1970s.

At present, Sikh councillors are in prominent numbers in local councils with concentrations of Sikh population. A number of councils, particularly in the South East (Greater London Area) have appointed Sikh lord mayors too. Piara Singh Khabra, became the first Sikh Member of Parliament representing Southall from 1994. Bradford produced the second Sikh MP, Marsha Singh, in 1997. Both Sikh MPs are Labour Party members. This year (1999), Tarsem Singh King, a Labour Party member from Sandwell in the Midlands, has been appointed the first Sikh in the House of Lords.

Balbir Singh was the first Sikh councillor on Bradford Metropolitian District Council; elected in 1986. Raghbir Singh Virdee succeeded him in 1994. At present (1999) there is no Sikh councillor in Bradford.

A number of Sikhs have contributed to the Bradford Bench as JPs. Mewa Singh Bassan was the first appointee in 1975 and the present author was appointed to the Bench in 1978. Since then fourteen others have served as JPs for various periods and seven of them are currently serving.

Despite the presence of these role models, the younger generation of Sikhs in Bradford show little interest in local politics and community relations institutions. Most of them seem to be preoccupied with self-advancement within their own careers. It would appear they are not even encouraged sufficiently to involve themselves in community affairs by their parents and the present leadership of the community organisations.

This is the case for all South Asian communities in Britain. Anwar (1998, pp 160-161) discovered that almost 50 per cent of young Asian people felt that Asian organisations do not recognise or do much to help with the problems of young Asians. According to him the situation seems to have become worse than in 1975 when only one in five had such feelings. Such feelings of alienation may partially explain the lack of young Asians' (including Sikhs) interest in political and community affairs in general.

CHAPTER 11

FIFTY YEARS ON

The processes of adjustment of Sikh migrants and the shaping of Sikh identity in the UK have been very much influenced by such factors as

- racial discrimination,
- restrictive immigration laws,
- minority group status,
- structural changes in the British economy and
- specific events in the Punjab.

These have constrained their choices between the strategies of assimilation, integration, confrontation and rejection in relation to mainstream society. At present they seem to have adopted different approaches for different aspects of their lives.

In employment 'assimilation' seems to be their obvious choice. The Bradford experience suggests that, unlike Muslims, whose priorities in education have been the maintenance and propagation of Islamic identity and religion, Sikhs have used education for economic self-advancement. Sikh parents have been more tolerant of their children's deviation from a traditional Sikh lifestyle and religious identity, in order to facilitate their progress in education and employment.

Many first generation Sikhs in Britain have started observing outward symbols of religious identity, such as beards and turbans. This is primarily to enhance self-esteem, self-improvement and to earn respect and status within their own community.

First generation Sikhs, 'the immigrant generation', are ageing fast. Despite their fairly long presence in this country they still feel uneasy about their inevitable-looking permanent stay in Britain. Most of them worked in a narrow band of jobs and many worked within 'ethnic work units'. They spent their leisure time with the family or in the company of other Sikhs. Their experience of the wider world outside their own community is extremely limited. Many of them, particularly women, are still living in their own social world. Their attitudes to life and living styles have very much changed from those with which they entered Britain but not changed enough to fully and comfortably accommodate the emerging life styles of their children, born and bred in Britain.

The younger generation is more exposed to the world outside their own community and to the competing value systems mediated through education. The impact on the younger generation of family structure, biradari, the British Punjabi Press, gurdwaras and other social organisations, the traditional internal control mechanisms of the community, is very weak. The variation in their attitudes and behaviour is a combination of generation gap and different cultural patterns of upbringing here. However, these differences do not always result in confrontation between parents and their children. Children seem to be re-examining certain aspects of their traditional culture and are redefining basic concepts like authority, happiness, morality, obligation, family, izzat (honour) and so on, to suit their new social environment. They appear to hold respect for traditional values but do not display a total commitment to the traditional Sikh way of life. Their parents, on the other hand, are trying to find a compromise solution. The present 'British Punjabi culture' is a clear blend of traditional Punjabi and contemporary British values.[1]

At a general level, the impact of local traditions on the Sikh community is pretty obvious. For example, at Christmas, it is not unusual to find glittering Christmas trees in many Sikh homes. Sending Christmas greetings to relatives and friends is common, whilst the exchange of Diwali or Gurpurb greeting cards is still an exception. The celebration of birthdays and wedding anniversaries is becoming increasingly popular, and is no longer a middle-class phenomenon. Sikh wedding ceremonies are becoming an interesting mixture of local and traditional South Asian rites and rituals. Interestingly, the conventional pattern of marriage arrangements and death ceremonies are least affected. It is the passage of time and, more significantly, the growing up of their children in a British environment which have brought about these changes.

Fifty years on, most Sikhs are enjoying a decent standard of living in Britain. Their economic success is self-evident. Despite some conspicuous changes in their economic values and consumption patterns, they are actively trying to preserve and propagate vital components of their traditional cultural and religious identity.

Sikh politics are still inwardly tilted and very much influenced by the political and religious events of the Punjab. British Sikhs are very much preoccupied with the internal conflicts and politics of gurdwaras. Topics of intense discussion in Sikh mehfals include: the management of local gurdwaras, community events, the effects of internal feuds and divisions in the community, character assessments of individual leaders, religious dogmas and fanaticism, negative assessments of granthis, religious preachers, sants and keertani jathas. Most leaders are very judgmental at a personal level. Very rarely are the affairs and achievement of others evaluated objectively and positively. More often, the lives and conduct of others are commented upon in negative, sensational, jealous and, sometimes, damaging ways.

Political and religious Sikh leaders in the Punjab maintain very close regular links with the British Sikh community and its leadership for their own, often selfish, reasons. However, as an unfortunate consequence of these links, the Sikh community in Britain remains divided on the same bases as in Punjab. For instance, in September this year (1999), Des Pardes, the most widely read British Panjabi weekly, carried full page advertisements by contenders from Punjab in the Parliamentary Election in India seeking financial support. Furthermore, the Shromini Akali Dal and the Indian Congress Party advertisements pleaded with British Sikhs to encourage their contacts in Punjab to vote for their candidates.

Changed Priorities

The subjects of mehfal discussions at different points clearly reflected the immediate priorities of Sikh migrants. Topics of conversation in mehfals of the 1950s-1970s used to be predominantly work related: the weight of individual pay packets, overtime availability, the nature and pleasantness of jobs and a general critique of managers' and supervisors' behaviour. There were exaggerated accounts of their remittances and investments back home. Information was shared about illegal ways of remitting money, methods of evading income tax and techniques of obtaining false documents about fake dependants.

Nostalgic feelings of happy experiences, bitterness about Indian officialdom and the frustrations of earlier life were exchanged in attempts to smooth over the hard realities and pains of their new life. Plans and arrangements about bringing into Britain their immediate families were sorted out, as were schemes of sponsoring other relatives and friends. The conversations were usually limited to individual aspirations, concerns and experiences. The world beyond the place of work, pub, lodgings and family left behind did not seem to exist. Little time was ever spent in discussing local or national politics beyond anti-immigrant news and views.

Over a period of the last two decades, the 'myth of return' is almost shattered. However, the interaction between the Sikh community in Britain and their families in Punjab has increased in the 1990s. A number of factors have contributed to an intensified movement between Britain and Punjab. The cost of air travel has remained fairly stable over the years and now appears modest and affordable. Presently, unemployed and retired men can afford an extended visit. The sorting out of investments made in the earlier years of immigration and interests in family properties require more frequent visits. People have started making even short visits, not lasting more than two weeks, to do shopping in India, particularly for weddings in order to get clothes and jewelry of the latest fashions and designs at much lower prices. This is a most convenient and efficient way of spending incomes generated by their investments in the earlier years of emigration, as such incomes are difficult to transfer to Britain through normal banking channels.

The flow of family members and relatives from Punjab, visiting to attend family social functions, has increased. Coming to Britain for a holiday has become an attraction as once they are here they are normally looked after by their relatives and friends. At the same time, many of them attempt to earn the cost of their trips by doing some casual work.

View of Home from Vilayat

With the increase in visits to Punjab, the experiences of journeys to and within India are a popular topic for gossip. Thus mehfals of the 1990s largely focus on the experiences of "home visits" and contemporary social issues concerning Sikhs in Britain. The stories of the adequacy or lack of appropriate in-flight services, troublesome travel from Delhi airport to their destination in Punjab, the increase in road traffic, the risks and dangers from the non-observance of traffic rules, the intolerable increase in noise and air pollution in their home cities, are frequently shared. The consciousness of environmental issues and problems of increasing pollution in their country of emigration is a new dimension in their thinking.

On the basis of their personal encounters with government officials they deplore the all pervasive bribery, corruption, idleness, delay, arrogance and lack of discipline in public offices. They are highly critical of the time consuming, harassing and outdated bureaucratic practices of identity checks in banks and at Delhi airport. Officials' lack of courtesy and good manners in dealing with the public astonishes them; whilst the rogue practices of travel agents which they happily tolerated at their point of immigration now annoy them the most. Interestingly, their nostalgic view of the home situation is replaced by a serious critique of life in Punjab. Such a critical and largely negative appraisal of contemporary official practices in India is based on their new experiences of dealing with officials in the public services in Britain.

Migrants' feelings of love for, and their eagerness to help with, the difficulties of their families left behind have been replaced by a serious criticism of their relatives' actions and attitudes. They discuss how their farming property and rented houses are proving headaches; they grumble about the unwillingness of their relatives and family members to pay any rents for the cultivation of their land or to release their possessions. On the contrary, family members demand money for the repair of ancestral homes and the upkeep of their other household possessions. Such concerns are expressed by most and people talk frankly and more frequently about their plans to sell their share in family farming land or property.

Migrants view the traditional notion of family and prestige quite differently now. Without any shame to the family name, they express their feelings of hurt and frustration at the lack of gratitude shown by their immediate family and relatives for the presents and generous contributions they have received towards the costs of family weddings, education of children and care of parents. The failure or unwillingness of relatives to return the long term interest-free loans, received so happily for improving their economic opportunities and social lifestylse, are now major causes of internal feuds between migrants and their relatives in Punjab.

The cultural scene in the Punjab has changed so much since the mid 1950s and early 1960s, the peak period of emigration to Britain, that the migrants visiting home are perceived with some curiosity by the native Punjabis. Visitors are made to feel like outsiders, despite their own belief that they have become more modern and advanced than those they left behind.

The experience of earlier established Sikh communities in countries such as Fiji, Singapore, Malaysia, British Columbia and Australia, suggests that despite their liberal religious traditions, it is doubtful if Sikhs will ever be completely assimilated into the mainstream of British society. The liberal, undogmatic and socialistic traditions and practices of Sikhism facilitate the processes of preserving their distinctive socio-religious identity. With the development of equal opportunity policies and multicultural education in Britain the outside pressures for change have lessened. Most Sikhs still live in a close-knit community that reinforces traditional values alongside the powerful role which gurdwaras play in propagating Sikh identity and Punjabi culture.

Most Sikhs are likely to maintain close links with the Punjab and the Sikh Diaspora. These links keep them socially and psychologically close to their roots. However, recent years have witnessed a change in the nature and strength of these links.

Despite the visits to the Punjab becoming shorter, they are more frequent. Again, despite their current display of deep feelings of alienation from their roots in the Punjab, partly caused by the events of 1980s and the growing coolness in the reception they get from their own families and relatives, links with Punjab are likely to continue for at least another generation. It can be argued that, fifty years on, their changed view of the "native home" (Punjab) suggests that, for most of them returning to the Punjab for permanent settlement is out of question. They are here to stay as British citizens.

NOTES

Chapter 1

1.   It started with the publication of Salman Rushdie's novel, *The Satanic Verses* in 1988. The British Muslims demanded a ban on the sale of the book and burnt copies of the book in public, first in Oldham and then in Bradford in February 1989. Some of their demonstrations resulted in violent incidents. Two chief concerns emerged during the debate on these events. First, that banning the sale and publication of a book amounts to denying an individual citizen the 'right of free speech', the most cherished principle of the western democratic system. Therefore, in demanding a ban on the book, Muslims were accused of being " un-British". The second concern arose from their perceived support for the 'fatwa' issued by the late Ayatollah Khomeini of Iran, pronouncing the death sentence for Salman Rushdie. Supporting the fatwa or a public threat to execute a death sentence on a British Citizen imposed by a foreign authority was interpreted as disloyalty to the British legal system.

During the 1990 Gulf Crisis, when British and American forces were sent into Saudi Arabia to protect her from an attack by the forces of President Saddam Hussain of Iraq, some British Muslim organisations which included the Bradford Council of Mosques demanded withdrawal of British and American forces from Saudi Arabia, the holy land of the Muslims. In doing this, British Muslims appeared to challenge the political decision of the British Government.

The establishment of a Muslim Parliament in Britain in 1991 again questioned the loyalty of British Muslims. This was understood to be promoting the notion that Muslims should be treated as a separate community subject to their own code of domestic law. The speeches of Dr. Kalim Siddique, the main force behind its establishment, raised serious concerns in the British media about the integration of British Muslims into mainstream British institutions. He vehemently argued against Muslims' integration into what he referred to as 'corrupt bog land of Western culture'.

2.   The earliest of these incidents was in the 1960's when Sikhs started their campaign to get recognition for their right to wear a turban. The campaign started with the local bus companies in Wolverhampton and Manchester refusing to employ turbaned Sikhs. The overall response of the authorities and the public was very much summed up in an editorial of the Telegraph & Argus, (6 October 1966), "if a man feels so strongly about the turban he should remain in the community where his views are shared". After a hard and prolonged campaign resulting in large demonstrations in all cities of Sikh concentration, with one of the leading campaigners fasting unto death and threatening to commit suicide by pouring petrol over himself, Sikhs eventually won the right to wear turbans as a part of the uniform. The turban issue emerged once again when a headmaster in the Midlands refused a Sikh pupil permission to wear his turban to meet the school's uniform requirements. It resulted in a nation-wide campaign and eventually the case was taken to the Lords and won (Mandla v Dowell Lee, House of Lords, 1983). The Sikhs had to fight equally hard, all over again, to win exemption from wearing a crash helmet over a turban when riding a motorcycle (Motor-Cycle Crash Helmets (Religious Exemptions) Act 1976). More recently, the Employment Act 1989 (Section 11) has exempted turban-wearing Sikhs from any legal requirement to wear safety helmets on construction sites.

3. These events included the Indian army attack on the Golden Temple in Amritsar. The Amritsar incident was followed by the assassination of the Indian Prime Minister, Mrs Indira Gandhi. A prominent Sikh leader in Britain (Dr. Jagjit Singh Chauhan) was shown distributing sweets at the news of her death in Southall. Her assassination triggered the mass killing of Sikhs in many Indian cities including Delhi.

Chapter 2

1. Guru Nanak in *Majh Ki War*, in *the Guru Granth Sahib*.

2. Guru Nanak in Tilang, in *the Guru Granth Sahib*.

3. It has been an established tradition to eat *Guru Ka Langar in pangat*, that is, sitting in rows on the floor of a gurdwara dining-hall. The tradition changed in the Sikh Diaspora, tables and chairs became a norm in the *langar* halls in most gurdwaras. However, this new practice was challenged in 1998, initially in some gurdwaras in Canada but, very quickly, it became a major controversial issue in all gurdwaras in the Diaspora. As a consequence of this, the *Jethedar* of the *Akal Takhat* in Amritsar, issued a *Hukamnama* (a religious edict) in April 1998 requiring all gurdwaras to serve *langar in pangat* and to remove chairs and tables from the dining areas. The Sikhs living outside India seriously questioned the necessity, rationality and validity of the *Hukamnama*. Its observance so far is partial.

4. The Maharajah Duleep Singh Trust in Thetford has erected a life-size bronze statue of Maharajah Duleep Singh. Prince Charles, the Prince of Wales unveiled the statue on 29 July 1999.

Chapter 3

1. The Labour Force Survey of Spring 1995, LFS, Office for National Statistics

2. See Policy Studies Institute's national survey by Modood et al., 1997, p 17.

3. See Smith, 1976, pp 202-203.

4. See Singh, 1980 and Ram, 1983, p 32.

5. See Smith, 1976, p. 204 and Brown 1984, p 4

6. Hiro, 1991; Rose, 1969; Aurora, 1967, chap 4, and James, 1974, pp 5-14 provides a useful general introduction to the migration of Sikhs into Britain and other parts of the world.

7. According to Bradford Metropolitan Council (1977, p. 30) of the total stock of houses in Bradford, 15 per cent were back to back houses and 47 per cent terraced.

8. In the early years of migration the success of an immigrant was judged in terms of him building a pucca house (brick-built) and buying land in his village. This is exactly what most Sikh migrants did in the 1950s through 1970s. However, they have started to experience difficulties in maintaining property titles, in collecting rents from users and even in taking possession of their inherited family

properties as well as those created through remittances.

9.   See Butterworth, 1968, p 144.

10.   Kalsi, 1992, provides very detailed and useful information on the caste-based social divisions and on Sikh sects in his publication.

11.   For further information on the Nirankari movement see, Akbar, 1985, pp 192-193 and Singh, K, 1964, p 51.

Chapter 9

1. See Ghuman, 1994 for Birmingham school children's and parents' views on the use of community languages.

2. Bradford Metropolitan District Council, Information and Planning Unit, 1995-1997 Examination Results, GCSE and A Level.

Chapter 10

1. These situations are explained in Chapter 7 on Transformation in Sikh Identity.

2.   For instance, displayed all around the walls of a hall of Guru Gobind Singh Gurdwara in Bradford are large pictures of incidents of historical persecution of Sikhs and the main Sikh martyrs. Such exhibitions are common in most gurdwaras in Britain.

Chapter 11

1. Anwar (1998), Singh (1987) and Thompson (1974) provide a good discussion about the attitudes of younger people and the shaping of a new Punjabi culture in Britain.

APPENDIX

Record of Office Bearers in the Management Committees of the Gurdwaras in Bradford

The information about the honorary officers of the Bradford Sikh organisations in this appendix has been collated with the help of the officers currently holding positions in the management committees concerned. Although every effort has been made by these officers to check the information from gurdwara records, yet some discrepancies are possible, as the records are not adequate and well maintained. In some cases, when a committee changed after an election or due to an internal dispute, previous records were not passed on to the new officers.

Ramgarhia Sikh Temple (Bolton Road)

Year	President	General Secretary	Treasurer
1979-82	Gurdial Singh Chana	Dhian Singh Bharaj	Arnarik Singh Sembi
1981-83	Gurdial Singh	ChanaDhian Singh Bharaj	Joginder Singh Riyat
1983-84	Dhian Singh Bharaj	Avtar Singh Ghataore	Joginder Singh Riyat
1984-85	Santokh Singh Bhogal	Rajinder Singh Panesar	Joginder Singh Riyat
1985-86	Jasbir Singh Kundi	Rajinder Singh Panesar	Panninder Singh Sagu
1986-87	Jasbir Singh Kundi	Dhian Singh Bharaj	Dalbir Singh Kundi
1987-89	Gurbax Singh Riyak	Rajinder Singh Panesar	Davinder Singh Kundi
1989-91	Gurbax Singh Riyat	Rajinder Singh Panesar	Surinder Singh Bansal
1991-92	Nirinal Singh Notay	Harphuman Singh Notay	Surinder Singh Bansal
1992-93	Pal Singh Panesar	Rajinder Singh Panesar	Surinder Singh Bansal
1993-94	Niranil Singh Notay	Rajinder Singh Panesar	Surinder Singh Bansal
1994-95	Niranil Singh Notay	Mangal Singh Sagu	Surinder Singh Bansal
1995-97	Niranil Singh Notay	Rajinder Singh Panesar	Surinder Singh Bansal
1997-98	Niranil Singh Notay	Mangal Singh Sagu	Balwant Singh Lal
1998-99	Pal Singh Panesar	Rachhpal Singh Flora	Balwant Singh Lal

Gurdwara Singh Sablia (Grant Street)

Year	Chairman	General Secretary	Treasurer
1994-95	Mohinder Singh	Parvinder Singh	Avtar Singh
1995-96	Rachlipal Singh	Parvinder Singh	Avtar Singh
1996-99	Tarsem Singh Dosanjh	Parvinder Singh	Balvinder Singh

Guru Nanak Gurdwara (Wakefield Road)

Year	President	General Secretary	Treasurer
1970-76	Karam Singh Kang	Mewa Singh Bassan	Mohinder Singh Cheera
1976-77	Santokh Singh Notay	Santokh Singh Bhogal	Joginder Singh Pabial
1977-81	Gurbachan S Panesar	Joginder Singh Pabial	Balwant Singh Lal
1981-82	Bishan Singh	Niranjan Singh Chahal	Pritam Singh Gill
1982-83	Bishan Singh	Rachhpal Singh / Harjinder Singh	Dalip Singh Bassan
1983-84	Hardip Singh	Harbans Singh	Gurdev Singh
1984-86	Bishan Singh	Harjinder Singh	Karam Singh Aujla
1986-88	Charanjit Singh Rehil	Sardara Singh Madhada	Gurmit Singh Hayer
1988-93	Mewa Singh Bassan	Gurmit Singh Hayer / Hardip Singh	Darshan Singh Garcha
1993-98	Piara Singh Mjhar	Harinder Singh Kang	Nirmal Singh Auffia
1998-99	Hardip Singh	Hajinder Singh	Gian Singh Auffia

Guru Ravidas Bhavan (Brearton Street)

Year	President	General Secretary	Treasurer
1982-84	Gurbachan Singh Mal	Ram Chand Bagga	Piara Ram Mehmi
1984-87	Ram Chand Bagga	Rattan Pal	Piara Ram Mehmi
1987-91	Jamail Ram	Rattan Pal	Piara Ram Mehmi
199P94	Ram Chand Bagga	Ashok Kumar	Piara Ram Mehmi
1994-97	Ram Chand Bagga	Vinod Kumar	Piara Ram Mehmi
1997-99	Ram Chand Bagga	Ram Murti Sallan	Piara Ram Mehmi

Amrit Parchar Dharinik Diwan

Year	President	General Secretary	Treasurer
1982-87	Pritam Singh	Sarwan Singh	Piara Singh Kang
1987-99	Pritam Singh	Sarup Singh	Jagtar Singh

The United Sikh Association

Year	President	Secretary	Treasurer
1964-65	Tara Singh Kohli	Ranjit Singh/ Gurmail Singh Sodhi	Karam Singh Kang
1965-66	Sardara Singh	Ramindar Singh	Harchand Singh/Chanan Singh
1966-67	Sohan Singh Sahota/ Ranjit Singh	Sadhu Singh Dhesi	Chanan Singh
1967-69	Ranjit Singh	Sadhu Singh Dhesi	Bakhshish Singh
1969-70	Sadhu Singh Dhesi/ Karam Singh Kang/ Amar Singh	Gurmail Singh Sodhi	Chanan Singh

Guru Gobind Singh Gurdwara, Gobind Marg (off Leeds Road)

Year	President	General Secretary	Treasurer
1970-76	Sadhu Singh Dhesi	Ranjit Singh Sangha	Chanan Singh
1976-77	Awar Singh Sandhu	Sarwant Singh Dosanjh	Chanan Singh
1977-79	Kulbir Singh Hayer	Parminder Singh Bains	Avtar Singh Kang
1979-81	Harbhajan Singh Rai / Darshan Singh Binnig	Joginder Singh	Balbir Singh Basi
1981-83	Sadhu Singh Dhesi	Ranjit Singh Sangha	Avtar Singh Basi
1983-85	Balbir Singh Basi	Ajit Singh Lall	Kulbir Singh Hayer
1985-87	Gurmit Singh Gill	Tarsem Singh Dosanji	Sadhu Singh Chhokar
1987-89	Ranjit Singh Sangha	Narinder Singh Manak	Balbir Singh Basi
1989-91	Satnam Singh Atwal	Harbans Singh Khaira	Sadhu Singh Khaira
1991-93	Tarsem Singh Dosanjh	Rashpal Singh	Amrik Singh
1993-95	Gurmit Singh Dhami	Harbans Singh Khaira	Raghbir Singh Sangha
1995-97	Gurmit Singh Dhami Ajit Singh Lall	Ranbir Singh Rai	Sadhu Singh Chhokar
1997-99	Gurmit Singh Gill	Sadhu Singh Chhokar	Kuldip Singh Gill
1999-00	Manjit Singh Gosal	Harpal Singh Javanda	Gurdial Singh Chattha

GLOSSARY

Panjabi words and phrases used in a particular context are described where they occur in the main text. Words and phrases used more frequently are briefly described below for the convenience of readers.

Adi Granth - Granth Sahib the Sikh scripture compiled by Guru Arjan, in 1604 AD. Also used interchangeably with the Guru Granth Sahib.

Akal Takht - The Eternal Throne, building facing the Golden Temple in Amritsar where Sikhs gather for political purposes.

Akhand Path - Continuous reading of the Guru Granth Sahib from beginning to end.

Amrit - Sanctified liquid made of sugar and water, used in initiation ceremonies.

Amrit Sanchar - Sikh rite of initiation into the Khalsa.

Ardas - The formal prayer offered at most religious acts.

Bani or *(Gurbani)* - Compositions in the Guru Granth Sahib.

Biradari - A social network of relatives or people beyond the family boundaries generally of the same caste within which mutual exchange of gifts on social events take place.

Dasam Granth - The collection of compositions of the tenth Sikh guru, Guru Gobind Singh.

Dupata - A big flowing scarf worn by most Punjabi women over their head.

Gaddi - Position of Guruship.

Granthi(s) - Reader(s) of the Guru Granth Sahib who officiate(s) at religious ceremonies.

Gurdwara - The doorway to the Guru (Guru's house), Sikh place of worship.

Gurmukhi - From the Guru's mouth: name given to the script in which the scriptures and Panjabi language is written.

Gurpurb - Celebration functions of Sikh gurus' birth or death anniversaries. Term also used for anniversaries of other important events in Sikh history.

Guru Granth Sahib - The Adi Granth completed by Guru Arjan Dev.

Guruship - The position of being a Guru.

Halal - Meat prepared in a ritual way (generally by Muslims).

Harimandar -	The Golden Temple, the gurdwara situated in the middle of the sacred pool at Amritsar.
Izzat -	Honour, respect or status of a family or an individual
Kabadi -	A popular game originally played in Punjabi villages in India and Pakistan.
Kachcha -	Specially designed underpants, one of the five K's (symbols of Sikh identity).
Kameez -	Top-dress worn by Punjabi women.
Kangha -	Comb worn in the hair as one of the five K's (symbols of Sikh identity).
Kara -	Steel band worn on the right wrist, one of the five K's (symbols of Sikh identity).
Karah Parshad -	Sanctified sweet food distributed at the end of Sikh religious ceremonies.
Kaur -	Princess, name given to all Sikh females by Guru Gobind Singh.
Keertan -	Devotional singing of the compositions found in the Guru Granth Sahib.
Keertani Jatha -	A group of musicians who sing hymns from the Guru Granth Sahib.
Kes -	Uncut hair, one of five K's (symbols of Sikh identity).
Khalsa -	Sikh community – literally meaning the community of the pure.
Khalsa Panth -	*The whole community of Sikhs following the code of* discipline prescribed by the Sikh gurus.
Khanda -	Double-edged sword used in the initiation ceremony and also an emblem on the Sikh flag.
Khatri -	*A Hindu caste, a step below the highest ranking Brahmans.*
Kirpan -	Sword, one of the five K's (symbols of Sikh identity).
Langar -	Guru's kitchen, the gurdwara-dining hall and the food served in it.
Pangat -	A row of people in the gurdwara dining hall sitting on the floor to have food.
Mehfal -	An informal social gathering generally held for poetry reading or entertainment.
Mela -	Fair, term used for festivals which are not gurpurbs.
Mulla -	A Muslim priest
Nagar Keertan -	Religious procession or a parade singing shabads (hymns).
Pandit -	A Hindu priest.

Panj Piaras -	The five beloved ones, first five Sikhs initiated into the *Khalsa* by Guru Gobind Singh - Five baptised Sikhs who take decisions in the sangat or who perform the Amrit Sanchar rite today.
Panth -	Sikh community.
Punjab -	Land of five rivers, area of India in which Sikhism originated.
Panjabi -	Language spoken in the Punjab.
Ragi-dhadi Jatha -	Group of musicians who generally sing ballads of Sikh historical events.
Rehat Maryada -	Sikh code of conduct.
Shalwar -	Baggy trousers worn by most Punjabi women.
Shabad -	Word, a hymn from the Guru Granth Sahib.
Sangat -	Congregation or assembly of Sikhs for worship in a gurdwara.
Sant -	The holy man or men.
Sant Sepahy -	Saint-Soldiers- the name given to the Sikhs organised by Guru Gobind Singh.
Sewa-	Service (physical, mental, financial) oftheSikh community, humanity in general and in a gurdwara.
Sikh-	Literally a learner or a disciple. A person who believes in the Ten Gurus and the Guru Granth Sahib and has no other religion.
Singh -	Lion, name adopted by all Sikh males.
Vaisakhi -	Name of a month and a major Sikh festival celebrating the formation of the Khalsa in 1699 AD.
Vilayt -	From England or Britain.

REFERENCES and BIBLIOGRAPHY

Akbar, M J (1985)   *India: The Seige Within -Challenges to a Nation's Unity;*
                                      Penguin.
Anwar, Muhammed (1976)   *Between Two Cultures: A study of relationshipsbetween*
                                      the generations in the Asian Community in Britain;
                                      Community Relations Commission.
Anwar, Muhammad (1998)   *Between Culture: Continuity and Change in the Lives of*
                                      Young Asians; Routledge.
Aurora, Gurdip Singh (1967)   *The New Frontiersmen;* Bombay, Popular Parkashan.
Ballard, Roger (1972/73)   *Family Organisations Among the Sikhs in Britain;*
                                      New Community, Vol 2, No1, pp 12-24.
Ballard, R and Ballard, C (1977)   *The Sikhs: The Development of South Asian*
                                      Settlements in Britain, in James L. Watson (Ed.)
                                      Between Two Cultures: Migrants and Minorities in
                                      Britain; Basil Blackwell.
Bhachu, Parminder (1980)   *Multicultural Education: Parental Views;* New
                                      Community, Vol XII, No1, pp9-12.
Bhachu, Parminder (1985b)   *Twice Migrants: East African Sikh Settlers In Britain;*
                                      Travistock Publications.
Bhachu, Parminder (1991)   *Culture, Ethnicity and Class Among Punjabi Sikh*
                                      Women in Britain; New Community, Vol 17, No 3,
                                      pp 401-412.
Boneham, Margaret A (1989)   *Ageing and Ethnicity in Britain: the Case of Elderly*
                                      Sikh Women in a Midland Town; New Community,
                                      Vol 15, No 3, pp 447-459.
Butterworth, Eric (1968)   *Muslims in Britain,* in A Sociological Yearbook of
                                      Religions in Britain, Book 2; SCM Press.
Bradford Metropolitan District   *District Trends;* BMDC.
   Council (1977)
Bradford Metropolitan District   *1995-1997 Examination results, GCSE and A Level,*
   Council (1999)   *Gender and Ethnic Group Analysis;* Information &
                                      Planning Unit. BMDC.
Bradford Metropolitan District   *Managing Cultural Diversity,* Directorate of Education.
   Council (1999)   BMDC.
Brown, Colin (1984)   *Black And White Britain, The Third PSI Survey;*
                                      Heinemann.
Dhir, Ranjit (1995)   *Pardes Nama* (Panjabi), Delhi, Navyug Publishers.
Drury, Beatrice (1991)   *Sikh Girls and the Maintenance of an Ethnic Culture;*
                                      New Community, Vol 17, No 3, pp 387-400.
Eames, Edwin and Robboy,   *The Wulfranian and the Punjabi: Conflict, Identity and*
   Howard   (1978)   *Adaptation;* Anthropological Quarterly, Vol Ll, No 4,
                                      pp 207-219.
Ghuman, P A Singh (1994)   *Coping With Two Culture,* Clevedon; Multilingual
                                      Matters Ltd.

Helwig, A W   (1979)

Hiro, Dilip   (1991)

James, Alan   (1974)
Jeffery, Patricia (1976)

John, De Witt (1969)
Josephides, Sasha (1991)

Kalsi, Sewa Singh (1992)

McLeod, W Hew (1997)
Modood, Tariq and Berthoud, Richard et al (1997)
Office for National Statistics (1995)

Peggie, A C W (1979)

Pettigrew, J (1972)

Ram, Sodhi (1983)

Ram, Sodhi (1984)

Rose, E J B et al (1969)

Sangha, Sujinder S (1997)

Singh, Khushwant   (1964)
Singh, Khushwant   (1999)

Singh, Ramindar   (1978)
Singh, Ramindar   (1979a)

Singh, Ramindar (1979b)

Singh, Ramindar (1980)
Singh, Ramindar and Green, Sebastian (1982)

Sikhs In England: The Development of a Migrant Community; Oxford University Press.
Black British, White British: A History Of Race Relations In Britain; Grafton Books.
Sikh Children in Britain; Oxford University Press.
Migrants and Refugees: Muslim and Christian Pakistani Families in Bristol; Cambridge University P.
Indian Workers Association in Great Britain; Oxford U. P.
Organisational Splits and Political Ideology in the Indian Workers Associations, in Werbner, P and Anwar, Muhammad (1991) Black and Ethnic Leaderships in Britain; Routledge.
The Evolution Of A Sikh Community In Britain; University of Leeds.
Sikhism; Penguin.
Ethnic Minorities In Britain: Diversity and Disadvantage; Policy Studies Institute.
The Labour Force Survey of Spring 1995; Office for National Statistics.
Minority Youth Politics in Southall; New Community, Vol Vll, No 2, pp 170-177.
Some Notes on the Social System of Sikh Jats; New Community, Vol 1, No 5, pp 354-363.
A Geographical Analysis of Indians in Bradford: Methods Used in Classifying Names on the Electoral Register, University of Leeds, p32.
A Geographical Analysis Of Indians In Bradford: Spatial Distribution and Temporal Trends 1971-81, Working Paper No 384; School of Geography, University of Leeds, Table 13, p 66.
Colour and Citizenship: A Report on British Race Relations; Oxforfd University Press.
Vilayton Vekhi Duniya (Panjabi); Birmingham, The Punjabi Guardian & Multi-Lingual Publishers
The Sikhs Today; New Delhi, Orient Longmans.
The Sikhs of the Punjab, in Stronge, Susan, The Arts of the Sikh Kingdom; V&A Publications
The Sikh Community in Bradford; Bradford College.
A Study of the Punjabi Press in Britain; The Asian, Vol 1, No 12, pp 7-10.
The British Election and the Punjabi Press; The Asian, Vol 11, No 2, pp 6-7.
The Sikh Community In Bradford; Bradford College.
Minorities In The Market Place: A Study of the South Asian and West Indian Shoppers in Bradford; National Consumer Council.

Singh, Ramindar (1985)   *The Education of Sikh Children and Youth in Bradford:*
                                        A Report on One Day Seminar; Bradford Sikh Parents
                                        Association.
Singh, Ramindar and Ram,   *Indians In Bradford: The Development of a Community;*
    Sodhi (1986)   Bradford & Ilkley Community College.
Singh, Ramindar (1987)   *Development of Punjabi Culture and Identity in Britain;*
                                        Coventry, Punjab Research Group.
Singh, Ramindar (1988)   *Sikhs in Canada: Some Observations, (in three parts);*
                                        The Punjabi Guardian, June-July.
Singh, Ramindar (1992)   *Immigrants To Citizens: The Sikh Community in*
                                        Bradford; Bradford & Ilkley Community College.
Singh, Ramindar (1994)   *Re-Evaluating the British Sikh Agenda,* The Sikh
                                        Reformer, Issue 5, pp 10-13.
Smith, David J (1976)   *The Facts of Racial Disadvantage: A National Survey;*
                                        PEP.
Tatla, Darshan (Ed) (1996)   *Bartania Vich Panjabi Bhasha* (Panjabi); Patiala (India),
                                        Publication Bureau Panjabi University
Taylor, J H (1976)   *The Halfway Generation: A Study of Asian Youth in*
                                        Newcastle-upon-Tyne, Slough; NFER Publishing Co.
Taylor, J. Monica and Hegarty,   *The Best Of Both Worlds . . . A Review of Research*
    Seamus (1985)   *into the Education of Pupils of South Asian Origin;*
                                        NFER-Nelson.
Telegraph & Argus, 16 June, 1964.
Telegraph & Argus, 12 August, 1964.
Telegraph & Argus, 6 October, 1966.
Telegraph & Argus, 14 November, 1968.
Telegraph & Argus, 28 August, 1980.
Telegraph & Argus, 26 March, 1998.
Telegraph & Argus, 12 January, 1999.

Thompson, Marcus (1974)   *The Second Generation--Punjabi or English;* New
                                        Community, Vol III, No 3, pp 242-248.
Watson, James L (Ed) (1977)   *Between Two Cultures: Migrants and Minorities in*
                                        Britain; Basil Blackwell.

Index of Names

A

Adi Granth 6, 7
Ajax Minerva Ltd 35
Akal Takhat 29
Akali Dal 17
Akbar, Emperor 6, 7, 15
Albion, The 34
Amrik Electronics 35
Amrit Parchar Dharmik Diwan 43, 44, 47
Amrit Parchar Dharmik Diwan Gurdwara 41, 49
Amritsar 6, 16, 30, 52, 63, 71
Anand Karaj 15
Anandpur Sahib 8
Anjana 91
Atwal, Harjinder Singh 63
Aurangzeb, Emperor 8, 16
Autoelectro 35
Awaze Quam 88

B

Baba Gian Singh Ji Johalanwale 43
Babbar Akali Movement 17
Bahadur Shah, Emperor 16
Bahadur, Banda Singh 16
Bani (sacred poetry) 5
Bassan, Mewa Singh 92
Bassi, B S 55
Bassra and Singh Solicitors 36
Belle Vue 34
Bhagat Singh 17
Bhai Bala 5
Bhai Mardana 5
Bhandal, Nirbhai Singh 61
Bharat Travel 36
Bhatoa and Patel 36
Bhatoa and Patel Grocery Warehouse 35
Bhogal, Nicky 35
Bhogal, Paul 35
Bhogal, Santokh Singh 35 Bhogal, Tony 35
Birmingham 21, 58, 59
Blanch Street 35
Blue Star Operation 30, 52, 71
BM Motors 36
Bolton Road 24, 41, 45, 59
Bolton ward 22
Bomanji, Lady 55

Boparai, Balbidur Singh 33
Boparai, Balbinder Singh 33
Bowling 22
Bradford Educational and Cultural Association of Sikhs 59, 61, 89
Bradford College 60
Bradford Council of Mosques 62, 84, 86
Bradford Festival (Mela) 91, 92
Bradford Moor 26
Bradford Moor ward 22
Bradford Muslim Parents' Association 85
Bradford North Parliamentary Constituency 22
Bradford Sikh Association 41
Bradford Sikh Parents' Association 59
Bradford Singh Sabha Gurdwara 46, 64
Bradford West Parliamentary Constituency 22
Breakfast TV News Extra 92
Brearton Street 41
British Kabbadi Federation 92
Bussan, Mewa Singh 63

C

Cartwright Hotel 34
Cemetery, The 34
Chana, Mohinder Singh 60, 63
Chapeltown Road, Leeds 39
Charities Commission 49
Cheema, Manjit Singh 63
Chigwell 85
Co-operative Hall 40
Commission for Racial Equality 57
Communist Party of India 55, 56
Coventry 55

D

Dalhousie, Lord 16
Dasam Granth 8
Delhi 16, 61
Department of Education and Science 85
Des Pardes 88
Dhaliwal, Govinder Singh 63
Dhand, Raghbir 88
Dhesi, Harbhajan Singh 57
Dhesi, Sadhu Singh 21